Living in Harmony with Nature

Living in Harmony with Nature

Vision Kunming- Montréal Global Biodiversity Framework

"By 2050, biodiversity is valued, conserved, restored and wisely used, maintaining ecosystem services, sustaining a healthy planet and delivering benefits essential for all people"

©Gloria Rodríguez Zuleta
2024

Legal Deposit 2024
Library and Archives Canada (LAC)
ISBN 978-2-9822899-1-8
Photo Covers: Spirit Island Jasper National Park AB Canada
©Glowing Earth

Living in harmony with Nature

Listening to the birds at home before sunrise

Breathing clean air

Admiring the colours of the flowers

Savouring fresh fruits, vegetables,

and healthy food

Drinking pure water

Learning

Working

Enjoying living creatures around us

Marveling at the beauty of sunset

following the movement of planets, and stars

at night

Being aware of happiness and peace

Everyone deserves it

Gloria Rodríguez Zuleta 2023

Dear Gloria:

Going through the pages of your book my heart goes back to the early years of our friendship around the sea, the discussions, the dreams, the thoughts of a cared and healthy ocean by all to all. It is so good to find that nothing in your words have been lost, the spirit still is there yet the threats humankind is posing to our planet. Your book reminds us on the messages of persons and joint efforts through the last century on the intents to cope with the urgencies to protecting nature. As long as we have persons, like you, being able to raise the call and remind the world the fantasy of nature, there will be hope.

Francisco A. Arias-Isaza

Preface

I salute the enthusiasm, perseverance and courage of the author Mrs Gloria Rodríguez Zuleta who, by this work, allows us to better know the individuals and collectives efforts done through the humanity recent history to improve our understanding of nature and its ecosystems, protect its life, and help to attain a sustainable and in harmony development.

This work describes the action of individuals strongly motivated who wrote scientific papers and books, founded associations and, from their efforts, conducted to the ratification of numerous international agreements.

We can follow the history and interaction of main world summits to support these agreements and to establish targets for ecosystem protection of lands and oceans, for the preservation of species diversity, and for mitigation of climate changes. Numerous references on internet sites complete with more details this overview.

In conclusion, the author suggests many ways and actions to individually improve our contribution to the well-being of our environment. The author invites us to increase our knowledge and link with nature and to marvel at its beauty, diversity and ingenuity. This way, we will be more motivated to protect it and to undertake actions to provide a better sustainable environment for future generations.

Michel Besner

Contents

Introduction

Earth was formed 4,600 million years ago. The first single-celled organisms appeared in the ocean during the Precambrian era 3,600 million years ago. Since then, different kinds of plants and animals have been present on the planet. *Homo sapiens* appeared before the last ice age, about 100.000 years ago.

As humans they grew in numbers they moved all over the planet. Scientists, archaeologists, anthropologists, and palaeontologists have tried to establish the trends of millions of years by interpreting stone artifacts, geological data and animal bones.

The wonder of the ice age artists inside the prehistoric art galleries, show evocative scenes of bison, buffalos, deer and horses as they observed the beauty of the wildlife that they depended on for their survival. Their eloquent art preserved on the rough walls and ceilings of the ancient Lascaux and Altamira caves give us a clue to the depth of their feelings for the natural world.

By 8000 B.C. some hunter-gatherers began to establish settlements and construct shelters. "With tiny stone blades and grinding tools, they gathered and processed wild plants and worked clay to make containers, many of which were artfully decorated. Though they still relied on hunting for much of their food supply, soon they were cultivating large stands of grain". Since thenMother Earth has been transformed.

Humans have always depended on what nature has continuously offered them, for food, shelter, clothing and health.

From mountains to oceans, beside lakes and rivers, within deserts and forests, Indigenous People and local communities have used their traditional knowledge to live in harmony surrounded by nature.

From the dawn of agriculture 10,000 years ago through the Industrial Revolution, the world has dramatically changed:

- More than 44,000 species are threatened with extinction
- Half of the world's population now live in cities
- Development degraded environment
- By 2030, 575 million people could still be living in extreme poverty
- Global temperature is now more than 1.2°Celsius warmer than in the preindustrial time
- Wildfires and droughts are expanding while floods are increasing
- Hurricanes in the coming century are predicted to be more intense
- Carbon dioxide and other greenhouse gas emissions have raised temperatures, even higher in the poles
- More than a third of the world's remaining glaciers will melt before the year 2100

- 95% of the oldest thickest ice in the Arctic is already gone.

Passionate people, scientists, economists, world leaders, indigenous people, local communities, and youth have awakened us to the complex situations affecting our survival.

Milestone agreements between nations have been signed. During this millennium, significant momentum began to protect life on Earth. Four global challenges we are facing:

- Sustainable Development
- Conservation and protection of biodiversity
- Clean, healthy, and productive oceans
- Climate change

The aim of this publication is to present in simple language that can reach the minds and hearts of everyone from 8 years old, the important facts, meetings, and messages from passionate people, governments, and organizations.

This publication is divided into the following 7 chapters: 1. Passionate People, 2. First Agreements to Protect Life, 3. First World Conference on Environment, 4. Protection of Marine

Life, 5. Summits for Development and Conservation, 6. Conservation of Biological Diversity, 7. Climate Change.

Studying, learning, understanding, and most important, putting into practice all of the above will give us the ability to protect Nature and Live in Harmony with our Mother Earth.

Gloria Rodríguez Zuleta

1
Passionate People

London Protecting Birds 1922

At midday on summer day, on 20 June 1922, a group of visionary conservationists concerned about the plight of the world's birds gathered at the London home of the Chancellor of the Exchequer, Sir Robert Horne, then MP for Glasgow. There were: Dr T. Gilbert Pearson, cofounder and president of National Association of Audubon Societies (now National Audubon in the US); Frank E. Lemon, honorary secretary of the Royal Society for the Protection of Birds (now BirdLife in the UK); Jean Delacour, president of the Ligue pour la Protection des Oiseaux (now BirdLife in France); and P.G. Van Tienhoven and Dr A. Burdet of the Netherlands.

United by their passion for birds, the group decided that coordinated international action was the answer to the various threats birds faced. They founded The International Council for Bird Protection (ICBP).

As it was written in The 1922 ICBP Declaration of Principles "...by united action, we should be able to accomplish more than organizations working individually in combating dangers to bird-life." Their early concerns were: the protection of migrating birds, the identification and protection of the areas where birds congregate in large numbers, and the most important sites for threatened birds. In 1993 (ICBP) changed their name to BirdLife International.

Today BirdLife International is a global family of over 117 national Partners covering all continents, landscapes and seascapes of the Planet. Their network of over 2 million birders, scientists and local volunteers helps BirdLife to track, follow, analyze, conserve and understand every bird species in the world. They have over 13 million individual members and supporters and unify over 100 nature conservation organizations from across the planet.

Fontainebleau - Union to Protect Nature 1948

An autumn day, on 5 October 1948, 26 years after the foundation of The International Council for Bird Protection (ICBP), following an international conference in the French town of Fontainebleau, the International Union for the Protection of Nature (IUPN) was established in 1956, the organization changed its name to the International Union for Conservation of Nature (IUCN).

It was the first global environmental union, which brought together governments and civil society with a shared goal to protect nature. Its aim was to encourage international cooperation and provide scientific knowledge and tools to guide conservation.

© iunc.org

During their first decade, IUCN's primary focus was to examine the impact of human activities on nature. They flagged the damaging effects of pesticides and promoted the use of environmental impact assessments, which have since become the norm for many sectors and industries.

In 1964, IUCN established the IUCN Red List of Threatened Species™, which has since evolved into the world's most comprehensive data source on global extinction risk.

©iucnredlist.org

The following years, IUCN was fundamental to the creation of key international Conventions, including the Ramsar Convention on Wetlands (1971), the World Heritage Convention (1972), the Convention on International Trade in

3

Endangered Species CITES (1973) A summary of those are presented in the following chapter.

Since the foundation IUCN have played an important role in conferences for the conservation of nature. In 1999, as environmental issues continued to gain importance on the international stage, the UN General Assembly granted IUCN official observer status. Later in the 2000s, IUCN pioneered Nature-based Solutions: actions to conserve nature which also address global challenges such as food and water security, climate change and poverty.

Today, with the expertise and reach of more than 1,400 Member and over 18,000 international experts, IUCN is the world's largest and most diverse environmental network. We continue to champion Nature-based Solutions as key to the implementation of international agreements such as the Paris Agreement on climate change and the UN's Sustainable Development Goals.

Nature Conservancy 1951

The Nature Conservancy is a global environmental nonprofit working to create a world where people and nature can thrive.

Founded in the U.S. through grassroots action in 1951, The Nature Conservancy (TNC) has grown to become one of the most effective and wide-reaching environmental organizations in the world.

Their goals for 2030 are:

4

Tackling Climate Change
Protecting Ocean, Land and Fresh Water
Provide Food and Water

Thanks to more than a million members and the dedicated efforts of our diverse staff and over 400 scientists, they impact conservation in 79 countries and territories (37 by direct conservation impact and 42 through partners).

Fund raising for Conservation
WWW 1961

In April 1961, Victor Stolan warned about the destruction of habitat and wildlife in East Africa, pointed out the urgent need for an international organization to raise funds for conservation. The idea was then shared with Max Nicholson, Director General of British government agency Nature Conservancy, who enthusiastically took up the challenge.

Nicholson was motivated in part by the financial difficulties facing the International Union for Conservation of Nature (IUCN), and felt that a new fundraising initiative might help IUCN and other conservation groups carry out their mission. He drafted a plan in April 1961 that served as a basis for WWF's founding, which was then endorsed by the executive board of IUCN in a document known as the Morges Manifesto. 1980, IUCN, UNEP and WWF published the World Conservation Strategy, a seminal document that stressed the interdependence of conservation and development, and first coined the term "sustainable development". These documents have been the foundation of conservation efforts since and together with the Global Diversity Strategy (published in 1992 by UNEP, IUCN, and WRI) lay the foundations for the Convention on Biological Diversity, a global treaty for the conservation and sustainable use of biological diversity developed by UNEP with support.

11 million activists worldwide speak out to protect diversity of life on Earth. WWF's Russell E. Train Education for Nature Fonds was provided more that 2.800 grants to support further conservations leaders around the world

In 2022 WWF is the world's leading conservation organization, World Wildlife Fund works in nearly 100 countries to tackle the most pressing issues at the intersection of nature, people, and climate. They collaborate with local communities to conserve the natural resources we all depend on and build a future in which people and nature thrive.

Rachel Carson *La Primavera Silenciosa* 1962

"Those who contemplate the beauty of the earth find reserves of strength that will endure as long as life lasts." Rachel Carson *The Sense of Wonder* (1965)

Rachel began her career as an aquatic biologist in the U.S. Bureau of Fisheries, and became a full-time nature writer in the 1950s. Her widely bestseller books: *The Sea Around Us, The Edge of the Sea, Under the Sea Wind*, explores the whole

of ocean life from the shores to the depths. Later she turned her attention to conservation, especially some problems she believed were caused by synthetic pesticides. The result was the book *Silent Spring* (1962), which brought environmental concerns and spurred a reversal in national pesticide policy, which led to a nationwide ban on DDT and other pesticides. It also inspired a grassroots environmental movement that led to the creation of the U.S. Environmental Protection Agency.

In 1965, The Rachel Carson Council was founded as a national environmental organization envisioned by Rachel Carson to carry on her work after her death. They promote Carson's ecological ethic that combines powerful and credible science and health research with a sense of wonder, awe, imagination, creativity and feeling for the beauty and bounty of the world that surrounds us and of which we are a part, in order to build a more sustainable, just, and peaceful future.

Rachel Carson was posthumously awarded the Presidential Medal of Freedom by President Jimmy Carter

"The Mother of the Oceans"
Elisabeth Mann Borgese 1972

Known worldwide as "The Mother of the Oceans", Elisabeth Mann Borgese dedicated all her life to the understanding of

ocean matters, to the development of a constitution for the oceans and to the consideration of the oceans as a "great laboratory for the making of a new international order based on new forms of international cooperation and organization, on a new economic theory, on a new philosophy.

She was a passionate campaigner with her friend Arvid Pardo, ambassador from the tiny island of Malta, who in 1967 held his famous speech on the oceans before the United Nations: "the world's oceans and seabed should become the common heritage of mankind, and, in the interest of present and future generations, should be fostered and administered exclusively to peaceful ends."

Elisabeth was an active member of the Club of Rome, the World Academy of Arts and Sciences, and an associate member of the Third World Academy. She served as a consultant to UNEP, UNESCO, UNIDO, and the World Bank and her work was recognized with several prestigious honors. Professor Elisabeth Mann Borgese authored more than a dozen books and many research papers and editorials and was awarded several doctorates honoris causa. As a senior fellow at the Center for Democratic Institutions in Santa Barbara, California, she launched her ocean project which led to establishment of the Pacem in Maribus Conference series with PIM I in 1970 and the foundation of the International Ocean Institute in 1972.

The IOI enjoys special consultative status with the United Nations Economic and Social Council (ECOSOC) and consultative status at some of UN's Specialized Agencies and works to uphold and expand the principle of the common heritage as defined in the United Nations Convention of the Law of the Sea.

The mission of the IOI is to ensure the sustainability of the oceans as the "source of life", and to uphold and expand the principle of the common heritage of mankind as enshrined in the United Nations Convention on the Law of the Sea.

In 2022, for the celebration of its first fifty years, IOI launched the IOI Ocean Academy, aimed at delivering ocean knowledge to persons of all backgrounds and all interests via short, targeted online courses. IOI counted nearly 2000 IOI Alumni worldwide and an active IOI presence in nearly 40 countries and regions. IOI annually delivers a Master degree in Ocean Governance and a global portfolio of training courses in collaboration with recognized universities and learning centers. It plays a principal role in promoting Ocean Literacy through partnership in the globally science-based publications – the World Ocean Review Series –

Greenpeace

The Greenpeace journey started in 1972 in the early hours of a September morning. The plan for that first Greenpeace crew was to sail a rickety fishing boat to the Arctic Ocean to stop a US government nuclear test. It was to be, in the words of Greenpeace co-founder Irving Stowe, "A trip for life, and for peace."

"We want to live on a healthy, peaceful planet. A planet where forests flourish, oceans are full of life and where once-threatened animals safely roam.

Where our quality of life is measured in relationships, not things. Where our food is delicious, nutritious, and grown with love. Where the air we breathe is fresh and clear. Where our energy is as clean as a mountain stream. Where everyone has the security, dignity and joy we all deserve. It's all possible. We can't make it happen alone, but have no doubt: We can do it together". https://www.greenpeace.org/international/explore/about/about-us/

Conservation Internacional

Since 1987, Conservation International has worked to spotlight and secure the critical benefits that nature provides to humanity by:

• <u>Stabilizing Our Climate by Protecting and Restoring Nature</u>

• <u>Doubling Ocean Protection</u>

• <u>Expanding Nature-Positive Economies</u>

Combining fieldwork with innovations in science, policy and finance, Conservation International has helped protect more than 6 million square kilometers (2.3 million square miles) of land and sea across more than 70 countries. With offices in more than two dozen countries and a worldwide network of thousands of partners, it's reach is truly global.

"The Climate guardian" Christiana Figueres 2015

Courtesy/Treva: Ray llan

Ms. Christiana Figueres is an internationally recognized leader on global climate change. She was Executive Secretary of the United Nations Framework Convention on Climate Change (UNFCCC) 2010-2016. She directed the successful Conferences of the Parties in Cancun 2010, Durban 2011, Doha 2012, Warsaw 2013, and Lima 2014, and culminated her efforts in the historical Paris Agreement of 2015. With the French hosts, they had made sure the major negotiation obstacles were resolved before the start of the Agreement. Ms. Figueres had received notorious recognitions from governments, civil society, press, and journals. In 2015 Christiana was named Climate guardian <u>in 365 days</u>: Nature's 10.

After their tireless mission at the UN, Christiana and Tom Rivett-Carnac co-founded the <u>Global Optimism</u>, an organization focused on bringing about environmental and social change. Since 2019, they co-hosted with Paul Dickinson the podcast Outrage + Optimism, where every Thursday they explore the stories behind the headlines on climate change, talking to the change-makers turning challenges into opportunities. In 2020 Christiana Figueres and Tom Rivett-Carnac published *The Future We Choose: Surviving the Climate Crisis* . They both work closely with key campaigners supporting efforts to ameliorate the consequence of climate change, among them being Greta Thunberg, Al Gore,

Leonardo DiCaprio, His Holiness the Dalai Lama, James Goodall, David Attenborough, and Robert Redford.

"The Darwin of the 21st century"
Edward Osborne Wilson 2016

Beth Maynor Finch

In the address, Wilson laid out how "biological diversity is being irreversibly lost through extinction caused by the destruction of natural habitats." He made a plea for action and stated that "we are locked into a race. We must hurry to acquire the knowledge on which a wise policy of conservation and development can be based."
Edward Osborne Wilson (1929–2021) is widely considered one of the greatest natural scientists of our time. He was a pioneer in efforts to preserve and protect the biodiversity of our planet, receiving more than 150 international awards, including Pulitzer Prizes for his books On Human Nature and The Ants.

In September 1986, E.O. Wilson gave the opening address at the seminal convening of the National Forum on Biodiversity held in Washington, D.C. Hundreds of people attended the event and thousands more listened in via teleconference. International media introduced the term "biodiversity" into the collective vocabulary. People everywhere began to take note of the accelerated loss of species and their habitats. In the address, Wilson laid out how "biological diversity is being irreversibly lost through extinction caused by the destruction of natural habitats." He made a plea for action and stated that

"we are locked into a race. We must hurry to acquire the knowledge on which a wise policy of conservation and development can be based."
Wilson spoke about the urgent need for broader research and understanding of life on our planet to protect key species and avoid unintended destruction of the ecosystems that sustain us all.

In 2016, E.O. Wilson wrote Half-Earth: Our Planet's Fight for Life, in a bid to create a "moonshot" goal for humanity to join together and work toward ending the global extinction threat. Wilson introduced the principles of Half-Earth which argues that the situation facing us is too large to be solved piecemeal and proposes a solution commensurate with the magnitude of the problem: dedicate fully half the surface of the Earth to nature.

In 2021, E.O. Wilson passed away leaving a legacy of conservation action that will forever inspire the global movement to end the extinction threat.

Text excerpted from eowilsonfoundation.org/about-us/e-o-wilson/, with permission of the E.O. Wilson Biodiversity Foundation. Photo courtesy of Beth Maynor Finch.

2
First Agreements to Protect Life

1929 International Plant Protection Convention

The concept of international plant protection began in 1881, when five countries signed an agreement to control the spread of grape phylloxera, a North American aphid that was accidentally introduced into Europe around 1865 and that subsequently devastated much of Europe's grape-growing regions.
 The next major step was the International Convention for the Protection of Plants, signed in Rome in 1929, followed in 1951 by the adoption of the International Plant Protection Convention (IPPC) by the Food and Agriculture Organization of the United Nations.

The IPPC came into force in April 1952, superseding all previous international plant protection agreements. It was recognized by the 1989 Uruguay Round of the General Agreement on Tariffs and Trade as a standard setting organization for the Agreement on the Application of Sanitary and Phytosanitary Measures (the SPS Agreement).

In 1992 the IPPC Secretariat was established at FAO headquarters in Rome and began its international standard-setting program, which was adopted by FAO the following year.

1931 Protection of Whales

1In 1931, 26 countries, including Norway, Great Britain and the United States, concerned about the effects of commercial whaling, signed in Geneva, the Convention for the Regulation of Whaling, to prevent whale extinction. Germany, Japan, and Russia, refused to sign it.

Five years later, in 1936, the International Agreement for the Regulation of Whaling was signed in London. This agreement set whaling seasons in the Antarctic and banned whalers from hunting certain endangered species. Once again, Japan refused to abide by this agreement. During the next whaling season, 46,039 whales were killed in the Antarctic.

© iwc.int

The early agreements weren't working. A powerful institution was needed. The International Whaling Commission (IWC) was established in 1946 as the global body responsible for management of whaling and conservation of whales. IWC developed quotas for the numbers of whales and designated areas and times of the year when whalers could hunt.

In 1982, the IWC voted to ban commercial whaling beginning in 1986. Eight years after the moratorium began, the IWC established the Southern Ocean Whale Sanctuary -- the water that surrounds Antarctica -- where whales cannot be killed. It didn't, however stop Iceland, Japan, and Norway from hunting whales there.

Today the IWC has 88 member countries. The Commission's work is divided into five main areas: Science, Conservation, Aboriginal Subsistence Whaling, Whale Killing & Welfare Issues, Infractions, and Finance & Administration Committee. The Scientific Committee comprises approximately 200 of the world's leading cetaceans scientists who report to the Commission each year. New conservation concerns exist and the IWC work program now also includes bycatch & entanglement, ship strikes, ocean noise, pollution and debris, and sustainable whale watching. https://iwc.int/en/

1971 Ramsar Healthy Wetlands

In 1960, IUCN received and approved a proposal from Dr. Luc Hoffmann calling for an international program on the conservation and management of marshes, bogs and other wetlands. A conference in Camargue, France, was organized and attended by some 80 experts from 12 European countries and from Australia, Canada, Morocco and the United States.

After six more years of conferences, technical meetings, and behind-the-scenes discussions, it was in Ramsar, Iran, that Convention on Wetlands was signed on February 1971 by seven countries. It is the oldest multilateral international conservation convention and the only one to deal with one habitat or ecosystem type wetlands It   was originally contracted by seven countries when it came into force on 21 December 1975.

Wetlands are among the most diverse and productive ecosystems. They provide essential services and supply all our fresh water. Wetlands are indispensable for the countless benefits or ecosystem services that they provide humanity, ranging from freshwater supply, food and building materials, and biodiversity, to flood control, groundwater recharge, and climate change mitigation.

As of March 2022, there are 172 contracting parties and 2,437 designated sites covering 254,691,993 hectares (629,357,620 acres) The country with the most sites is the United Kingdom with 170.

1972 World Heritage Convention

The World Heritage Convention concerning the Protection of the World Cultural and Natural Heritage developed from the merging of two separate movements: the first focusing on the preservation of cultural sites, and the other dealing with the conservation of nature.

The most significant feature of the 1972 World Heritage Convention is that it links together in a single document the concepts of nature conservation and the preservation of cultural properties. The Convention recognizes the way in which people interact with nature, and the fundamental need to preserve the balance between the two

1973 Trade of Wild Fauna and Flora Animals and Plants ,CITES Washington

In the 1960's, there was widespread information about the endangered status of many prominent species, such as the tiger and elephants. Plus, it was vast trade of animals and plants and the array of wildlife products derived from them, including food products, exotic leather goods, wooden musical instruments, timber, tourist curios and medicines.

Levels of exploitation of some animal and plant species were so high that there was a need for an agreement between countries to safeguard these resources for the future. That is why, in 1963, members of the International Union for Conservation of Nature IUCN met to prepare it. Ten years later, a text of the Convention on International Trade in Endangered Species of Wild Fauna and Flora -CITES- was finally agreed at a meeting of representatives of 80 countries in Washington, D.C., United States of America, on 3 March 1973, and on 1 July 1975 CITES entered in force, CITES currently protects roughly 5,800 species of animals and 30,000 species of plants.

CITES currently protects roughly 5,800 species of animals and 30,000 species of plants.

1979 Convention on the Conservation of Migratory Species of Wild Animals (CMS) Bonn

In 1979, while whales, dolphins, rays, turtles and sharks swam in the ocean, elephants crossing forest and savanna searched for food and water, birds flew over continents, all of them in danger, an environmental treaty of the United Nations, the Convention on the Conservation of Migratory Species of Wild Animals (CMS) was signed in Bonn

An environmental treaty of the United Nations, the Convention on the Conservation of Migratory Species of Wild Animals (CMS) provides a global platform for the conservation and sustainable use of migratory animals and their habitats. This unique treaty brings governments and wildlife experts together to address the conservation needs of terrestrial, aquatic, and avian migratory species and their habitats around the world. Since the Convention's entry into force in 1979, its membership has grown steadily to include 133 Parties from Africa, Central and South America, Asia, Europe and Oceania.

657 Species

200Mammalia   385 Ave   10 Reptilia   Sturgeon   40 Shark & Ray.   Monarch Butterfly

3

First Conference on Human Environment Stockholm

iStock.com/Deejpilot

The first United Nations Conference on the Human Environment was held from 5 to 16 June in 1972 in Stockholm, Sweden.

The Conference was attended by 1,200 official delegates from 113 countries, as well as members of the specialized agencies of the United Nations. The Conference documents drew upon a large number of papers received from Governments as well as inter-governmental and non- governmental organizations, including 86 national reports on environmental problems.

United Nations Environment Program (UNEP) was created and the World Environment Day was established.

Two documents were adopted:

1.The Stockholm Declaration

The Stockholm Declaration, which contained 26 principles, placed environmental issues at the forefront of international concerns. It marked the start of a dialogue between industrialized and developing countries concerning the link between economic growth, the pollution of the air, water, and oceans and the well-being of people around the world

2.The Action Plan

The Action Plan contained 109 recommendations for the Global Environmental Assessment Programme, including activities carried out at the national and international levels

The following years of the Stockholm Declaration and the Action Plan, a number of global environmental challenges had not been adequately addressed.

In 1980 IUCN, UNEP, and WWF published the World Conservation Strategy. Living Resources Conservation for Sustainable Living which helped define the concept of 'sustainable development'.

I

In 1983, the Secretary General of the United Nations asked Gro Harlem Brundtland, then-President of Norway, to head up the World Commission on Environment and Development, charged with identifying the obstacles standing in the way of the nations of the world in pursuing sustainable development and recommending solutions.

After four years of research, the Commission released "Our Common Future," also known as "The Brundtland Report," concluding that economic development must become less

©Teigens Fotoatelier
Norsk Teknisk Museum

ecologically destructive. It said, "Humanity has the ability to make development sustainable – to ensure that it meets the needs of the present without compromising the ability of future generations to meet their own needs".

http://www.un-documents.net/our-common-future.pdf

The Brundtland Report called on the UN to establish the UN Programme of Action on Sustainable Development to carry out the directives outlined in the report. The publication of *Our Common Future* on October 1987 by the United Nation and the work of the World Commission on Environment and Development laid the foundations for the Rio Summit, held later in Rio de Janeiro in 1992

4
Protection of Marine Life

1608 "Freedom of the seas"

"Freedom of the seas" proposed by Dutch jurist Hugo Grotius in 1608, argued by the English academic John Selden in 1635 was for centuries the customs law in the Ocean.

Sailing boats hunted whales...Basque came from Europe to Canada to replenish their fishing boats with cod. Maritime powers traded from Africa to America and back to Europe...

Coastal States could only protect 3 miles reached by cannons from shore.

During the twentieth century jurisdiction, conservation and protection of Marine Life started:

In 1945, President Harry S Truman, unilaterally extended United States jurisdiction over all natural resources on that nation's continental shelf.

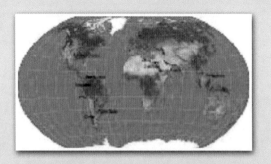

©commons.wikimedia.orgFile:Equal_Earth
projection Adaptado por Gloria Rodríguez

Argentina in 1946 claimed its shelf and the epicontinental sea above it. Chile and Peru in 1947, and Ecuador in 1950, asserted sovereign rights over a 200-mile zone, hoping thereby to limit the access of distant-water fishing fleets and to control the depletion of fish stocks in their adjacent seas.

Egypt, Ethiopia, Saudi Arabia, Libya, Venezuela, and some Eastern European countries laid claim to a 12-mile territorial sea Indonesia asserted the right to dominion over the water that separated its 13,000 islands. The Philippines did likewise.

1958 First United Nations Conference on the Law of the Sea

International community continued studies and meetings until 1958 when the first United Nations conference on the Law of Sea (UNCLOS I) was held in Geneva.

From 24 February to 27 April 1958, 86 states examined the technical, biological, economic, and political aspects of the law of the sea, as well as codified the results into an international convention or treaty.
 Four separate international conventions were adopted:

1. Territorial Sea and the Contiguous Zone
2. High Seas
3 Fishing and Conservation of the Living Resources of the
   High Seas
4. Continental Shelf

24

A second conference was held in 1960 at Geneva to consider topics which had not been agreed upon at the 1958 Conference.

The following years scientists, diplomats, and organizations related with the Ocean continue their proposals.

A third conference was held in New York in 1973.

Meanwhile, large fishing boats devastated marine life with trawl nets. Species began to show signs of depletion. In addition, ships and tankers transported harmful cargoes polluting and threatening all forms of ocean life.

1982 UNCLOS Montego Bay

Due to the complexity of the topics related with the Ocean, a third conference was convened in New York in 1973. Scientists, scholars, and world leaders worked tireless during 11 sessions the following year propose a more complex treaty including jurisdictions, fishery resources, mineral resources, marine science, technology, and environmental protection of life in the Ocean.

Meetings and reports continued until a final conference in Montego Bay, Jamaica. Finally, on December 10, 1982, the United Nations Convention on the Law of the Sea (UNCLOS) was signed by 117 States. The Convention entered into force in 1994.

Some of the key features of the Convention are:

Coastal States have sovereign rights in a 200-nautical mile exclusive economic zone (EEZ) with respect to natural resources and certain economic activities, and exercise jurisdiction over marine science research and environmental protection

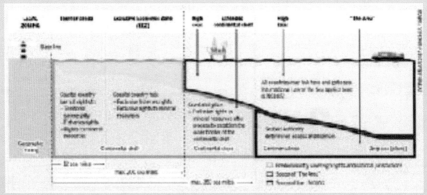

Coastal States have sovereign rights over the continental shelf (the national area of the seabed) for exploring and exploiting it; the shelf can extend at least 200 nautical miles from the shore, and more under specified circumstances

Archipelagic States have sovereignty over a sea area enclosed by straight lines drawn between the outermost points of the islands

Extended Coastal States, Islands, and Archipelagic States Maritime Zones within 200 EEZ

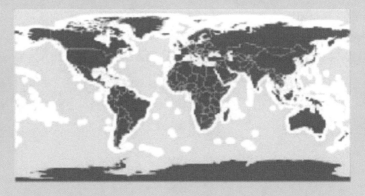

https://oceanexplorer.noaa.gov/facts/media/global-map-EEZs-hires.jpg

For the twentieth anniversary of UNCLOS, this review was published.

Marine life in the High Sea, however, was still not protected

The High Seas Treaty of Marine Biodiversity

On June 19th, 2023 in New York, 196 countries adopted by consensus a new treaty regulating the High Seas -Part VII- of UNCLOS: the 2023 Agreement under the United Nations Convention on the Law of the Sea on Conservation and Sustainable used of Marine Biological Diversity of Areas Beyond National Jurisdiction (BBNJ),

Scientists, Indigenous Peoples and local communities, civil society, academic, research institutions, and the private sector worked together to build this new International Treaty which aimed at better implementing the UNCLOS.

UN Secretary-General António Guterres touted the Agreement as a historic treaty and encouraged all member states to "spare no effort to ensure that this agreement enters into force.

Key points of the Agreement include:

• A procedure to establish large-scale marine protected areas in the high seas that facilitates the achievement of the target to effectively conserve and manage 30% of land and sea by 2030.

- Establishing the sharing of benefits from marine genetic resources and foresees capacity building and the transfer of marine technology among the parties.

- Clear rules to conduct environmental impact assessments, with the right checks and balances, before running activities in the high seas.

©NOAA

- The Agreement promotes the sustainable use of marine areas beyond national jurisdiction (BBNJ). These areas makeup over 60% of the world's ocean surface and are home to a diversity of living and non-living resources that provide a wide range of ecosystem services to support human wellbeing. Cooperation and coordination among organizations with independent mandates and interests in BBNJ will become increasingly important to achieve long-term common goals relating to the effective conservation of biodiversity and sustainable resource use.

Marine Observation Organizations

While UNCLOS and BBNJ agreements were negotiated to protect marine life, scientists were finding new marine species and identifying marine adaptability and resilience to climate change, fishing pressure and land-derived pollution. A global system was necessary to share their observation for the conservation of biodiversity and the management of human actions wisely.

Global Ocean Observing System (GOOS)

In 1991, the Global Ocean Observing System (GOOS) was created leading the development of a truly global ocean observing system that helps coordinate groups around the world to set requirements about the essential information needed for the sustainable development, safety, wellbeing and prosperity.

GOOS is led by the Intergovernmental Oceanographic Commission (IOC) of UNESCO, and is sponsored by the World Meteorological Organization (WMO), the United Nations Environment Program (UNEP) and the International Science Council (ISC).
GOOS is organized into Regional Alliances and a central coordinating office that led and support a community of international, regional and national ocean observing programs, governments, UN agencies, research organizations and individual scientists:

- Monitoring marine ecosystem health and preserving life
- Leading, coordinating and supporting vital ocean observing
- Modelling, mitigating and adapting to climate change
- Underpinning accurate weather forecasts and warnings

During the Decade of Discovery, with the $650 million donated by the Alfred P. Sloan Foundation, the First Census of Marine life was produced.   The program was implemented during 2000-2010 and then ended. 2,700 scientists from 80 nations participated, 6,000 new species of marine life were discovered, and 47 million distributions were recorded.

OBIS

In 2009, OBIS a global open-access data and information clearing-house on marine biodiversity for science, conservation and sustainable development, emanated from the Census of Marine Life (2000-2010). It was adopted as a project under IOC-UNESCO's International Oceanographic Data and Information (IODE).

Its VISION is to be the most comprehensive gateway to the world's ocean biodiversity and biogeographic data and information required to address pressing coastal and world ocean concerns.

Its MISSION is to build and maintain a global alliance that collaborates with scientific communities to facilitate free and open access to, and application of, biodiversity and biogeographic data and information on marine life.

There are more than 20 OBIS nodes around the world connecting 500 institutions from 56 countries. Collectively, by 2023, they had provided over 45 million observations of nearly 120,000 marine species, from Bacteria to Whales, from the surface to 10,900 meters depth, and from the Tropics to the Poles. The datasets are integrated so we can search and map them all seamlessly by species name, higher taxonomic level, geographic area, depth, time and environmental parameters.

In 2014, the Global Biodiversity Information Facility (GBIF) and the Intergovernmental Oceanographic Commission of UNESCO (IOC) /OBIS signed a collaboration agreement with the aims to improve the volume and quality of biodiversity information available to policy makers for conservation and sustainable use of the ocean's biological resources.

http://obis.org/2014/10/03/gbif/

Marine Biodiversity Observation Network (MBON)

In 2010, a group of scientists, managers, and agency representatives envisioned an operational Marine Biodiversity Observation Network (MBON) to catalyze increased and routine observations of life in the sea, to satisfy needs of society in a manner similar to what is done today for weather observations.

In 2014, US MBON received funds from three federal US agencies, the National Aeronautics and Space administration (NASA), the National Oceanic and Atmospheric Administration (NOAA), and the Bureau of Ocean Energy Management (BOEM), and partnered with Shell Oil through National Oceanographic Partnership Program (NOPP) for five year projects. The goal was to demonstrate that it is possible to have a single biodiversity observation system address the needs of multiple stakeholders, from local to national.

© MBON

In 2016, MBON entered into a collaborative process and partnership with GOOS, OBIS, and the global Group on Earth Observations Biodiversity Observation Network (GEO BON). GEO incorporated MBON as a thematic node.

The same year, GOOS, OBIS and GEOBON MBON signed a collaboration agreement to join efforts towards a sustained, coordinated global ocean system of marine biological and ecosystem observations to support management decisions and address relevant science and societal needs. OBIS plays a key role in fostering wider data sharing, curation and aggregation in order to streamline the feeding of integrated and quality-controlled datasets into models and forecasts.

The international MBON program is led by an Executive Secretary office located in the Azores (Portugal), and regional offices have been established in the Asia Pacific (AP MBON), in Europe, and in the United States. Additional regional partnerships are included under the MBON Americas Pole to Pole program.

Marine Life 2023

In 2021, over 60 private, government, academic, and civil society organizations teamed up to change the way that society understands and forecasts marine life. They organized the Marine Life 2030 program, endorsed by the United Nations Ocean Decade.

Its Vision is: "By 2030 and beyond, anyone, anywhere, will have access to information on marine species and ecosystems important to local fisheries, culture, health, and livelihoods. We will be able to diagnose how species are shifting with climate change and management interventions, to achieve a sustainable future for nature and people".

To accomplish it, as it stated in its website, Marine Life 2023, convene stakeholders to chart the course together, implementing equitable management for long-term coordination and financing of global marine life observation and applications, leverage emerging innovation to democratize marine life knowledge, using omics, acoustics, imaging, and AI, and a sequence-based Ocean Biocode of global marine species, integrate biodiversity into a global ocean observation system by establishing and promoting interoperable biodiversity standards and best practices, integrating with other disciplines, and apply enhanced knowledge of marine life to co-develop solutions, informing conservation and sustainable use of marine life by trained stakeholders in every coastal nation.

To fulfill its mission, Marine Life 2023 attracted Academic Partners, International Governmental Organizations, Non-Governmental Organizations, National Governments, as well as the Private Sector, and Project Representatives, who also provided core leadership in the co-design of Marine Life 2030 Program.

2021-2030 The Ocean Decade

The Ocean, 71% of the planet's surface, feeds us, protects us and absorbs more than 90% of the excess heat generated by global warming. Plus, 3 billion people depend on marine and coastal biodiversity for their livelihoods. That is why in 2017, the United Nations General Assembly proclaimed the 'Ocean Decade' to produce 'The Science We Need for the Ocean We Want', https://oceandecade.org/

The Ocean Decade enables countries to achieve all of their ocean-related Agenda 2030 priorities, guided by the United Nations Convention on the Law of the Sea (UNCLOS). Focusing on the Sustainable Development Goal 14, (which will be presented in the next chapter), the Ocean Decade leads to improved integrated ocean management and development of a sustainable ocean economy.

An equally transformational part of the Ocean Decade is about humanity and our relationship with the ocean. Understanding of the value of the ocean can be nurtured through ocean literacy. Holders of indigenous and local knowledge will work as essential partners of the Ocean Decade and will contribute to highlighting the multitude of cultural values of the ocean.

The 7 Ocean Decade Outcomes describe the Ocean We Want:

•A clean ocean where sources of pollution are identified and reduced or removed

•A healthy and resilient ocean where marine ecosystems are understood, protected, restored and managed

•A productive ocean supporting sustainable food supply and a sustainable ocean economy

•A predicted ocean where society understands and can respond to changing ocean conditions

•A safe ocean where life and livelihoods are protected from ocean-related hazards

•An accessible ocean with open and equitable access to data, information and technology and innovation

•An inspiring and engaging ocean where society understands and values the ocean in relation to human wellbeing and sustainable development

Ocean Decade Vision 2023

The Ocean Decade launched a strategic process, the Ocean Decade Vision 2023, to identify a common measure of success for each of the 10 Ocean Decade Challenges by 2030.

The Vision 2030 process is coordinated by IOC/UNESCO in its role and led by 10 expert Working Groups.These multi-stakeholder groups include representatives from Decade Actions, government, intergovernmental organizations, private sector, Indigenous and local communities, early career ocean professionals, non-governmental organizations, academia, and philanthropic foundations, representing diverse demographics and genders. They meet every three years. The first one was the Ocean Decade Barcelona Conference on April 10, 2024 where each challenge work was presented:

10 Years   10 Challenges   1 Ocean

 1 Understand and beat marine pollution

 2 Protect and restore ecosystems and biodiversity

 3 Sustainably feed the global population

 4 Develop a sustainable and equitable ocean economy

 5 Unlock ocean-based solutions to climate change

 6 Increase community resilience to ocean hazards

 7 Expand the Global Ocean Observing System

 8 Create a digital representation of the ocean

 9 Skills, knowledge, and technology for all

 10 Change humanity's relationship with the ocean

© oceandecade.org/challenges

5
Summits for Development and Conservation

1992 Rio Earth Summit

On the 20th anniversary of Stockholm the First Human Environment Conference in Stockholm, Sweden, in 1972, the

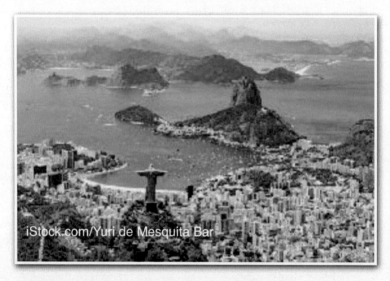

iStock.com/Yuri de Mesquita Bar

second UN Conference on Environment and Development was held from 3 to 14 June 1992 in Rio de Janeiro, Brazil.

Political leaders, diplomats, scientists, representatives of the media and non-governmental organizations (NGOs), from 179 countries met for a massive effort to focus on the impact of human socio-economic activities on the environment. A 'Global Forum' of NGOs was also held in Rio de Janeiro at the same time, bringing together an unprecedented number of NGO representatives, who presented their own vision of the world's future in relation to the environment

Severn Suzuki, speaking for "ECO" the Environmental Children's Organization touched the general meeting with her remarkable speech "I am here to speak -- speak on behalf of the starving children around the world whose cries go unheard. I am here to speak for the countless animals dying across this planet, because they have nowhere left to go...

https://www.youtube.com/watch?v=oJJGuIZVfLM&pp=ygUUc2V2ZXJuIHN1enVraSBzcGVlY2g%3D

At the Earth Summit two conventions were signed:

CBD

- The <u>United Nations Framework Convention on Climate Change</u>
- The <u>Convention on Biological Diversity</u>

Three documents were adopted:

- The **Rio Declaration** on Environment and Development
- The <u>Agenda 21</u>
- The <u>Declaration on the principles of forest management</u>

The **Rio Declaration** recognized the integral and interdependent nature of the Earth, our home and proclaims in the first Principle that "Human beings are at the centre of concerns for sustainable development. They are entitled to a healthy and productive life in harmony with nature".

The **Agenda 21** stablished a daring program of action called for new strategies to invest in the future to achieve overall sustainable development and the conservation and management of resources in the 21st century:

- Protection of the atmosphere
- The fight against deforestation
- The fight against desertification and drought
- Conservation of biological diversity
- The protection of the oceans, all seas and adjacent coastal areas
- Protecting the quality and supply of freshwater resources

The Global Environment Facility (GEF), worked since then to address the world's most challenging environmental issues. https://www.thegef.org/

The 'Earth Summit' concluded that the concept of sustainable development was an attainable goal for all the people of the world, regardless of whether they were at the local, national, regional or international level.

Two years later, in 1994, the first World Conference on the Sustainable Development of Small Island Developing States was held in Bridgetown, Barbados, and the United NationsConvention to Combat Desertification (UNCCD) was adopted in Paris.https://www.unccd.int/

2000 Millennium Summit New York

The Millennium Summit, held from September 6 to 8, 2000 at United Nations Headquarters in New York, was, at that time, the largest gathering of heads of state and government of all time.

iStock.com/OlegAlbinsky

It concluded with the adoption by the 189 Member States of the **Millennium Declaration**, in which the eight Millennium Development Goals (MDGs) were set out, by the target date of 2015.

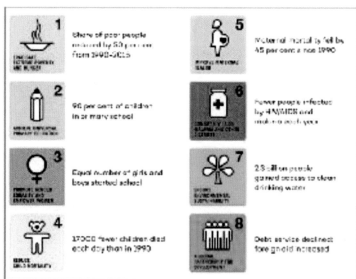

2002 Johannesburg Summit

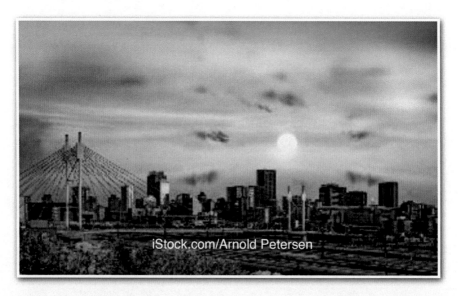

iStock.com/Arnold Petersen

From the 26th August until the 4th of September 2002 the World Summit on Sustainable Development (WSSD) was held in Johannesburg, South Africa. Around ten thousands participants, including heads of State and Government, national delegates and leaders from non-governmental organizations (NGOs), businesses and other major groups to focus the world's attention and direct action toward meeting difficult challenges, including improving people's lives and conserving our natural resources in a growing in population world, with ever-increasing demands for food, water, shelter, sanitation, energy, health services and economic security.

They adopted a <u>Political Declaration and Implementation Plan</u>

As it is written in the Declaration: "At the beginning of this Summit, the children of the world spoke to us in a simple yet clear voice that the future belongs to them, and accordingly challenged all of us to ensure that through our actions they will inherit a world free of the indignity and indecency occasioned by poverty, environmental degradation and patterns of unsustainable development".

Also the World Summit on Sustainable Development, called for the negotiation of an international regime, within the framework of the Convention   on Biological Diversity to promote and safeguard the fair and equitable sharing of benefits arising from the utilization of genetic resources.

2012 Rio+20 The Future We Want"

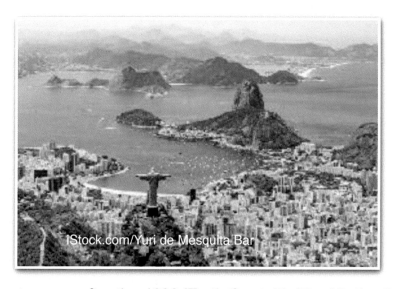

Twenty years after the 1992 'Earth Summit', Rio+20, the third UN Conference on Sustainable Development was hosted by Brazil in Rio de Janeiro. 192 UN member states, private sector companies, NGOs and other groups participated in this summit.

Thousands of non-governmental organizations (NGOs) and activists joined forces to stand up to what they said was exploitation and degradation of the Earth. The negation of the rights of indigenous people and the deforestation threatened Amazonian ethnic groups.

.

The member states approved the final document **"the future we want"**, in which:

- They recognized that planet Earth and its ecosystems are our home and that, to achieve a fair balance between the economic, social and environmental needs of present and future generations, it is necessary to promote harmony with nature.

- They called for holistic and integrated approaches to sustainable development that lead humanity to live in harmony with nature and lead to measures to restore the health and integrity of the Earth's ecosystem.

- They decided to launch a process to develop a set of Sustainable Development Goals (SDGs), based on the Millennium Development Goals (MDGs), which were adopted three years later at the Summit on Sustainable Development in New York.

2015 Millennium Development Goals Conference New York

At a three-day United Nation Summit on Sustainable Development, more than 150 world leaders gathered at United

Nations Headquarters in New York. They formally approved the 2030 Agenda for Sustainable Development, a new plan called **Transforming Our World.**

 The goal of the plan is to find new ways to improve the lives of the world's people, to eradicate poverty, to promote prosperity and well-being for all, to protect the environment, and to fight against climate change.

They recognize that ending poverty and other deprivations must go hand-in-hand with strategies that improve health and education, reduce inequality, and spur economic growth – all while tackling climate change and working to preserve our oceans and forests.

The 2030 Agenda for Sustainable Development by 2030, includes a declaration, 17 sustainable development goals and 169 targets. https://sdgs.un.org/es/goals

1: No Poverty
Economic growth must be inclusive to provide sustainable jobs and promote equality.
https://sdgs.un.org/goals/goal1

2: Zero Hunger

The food and agriculture sector offers key solutions for development, and is central for hunger and poverty eradication. https://sdgs.un.org/goals/goal2

3: Good Health and Well-Being

Ensuring healthy lives and promoting the well-being for all at all ages is essential to sustainable development. https://sdgs.un.org/goals/goal3

4: Quality Education

Obtaining a quality education is the foundation to improving people's lives and sustainable development. https://sdgs.un.org/goals/goal4

5: Gender Equality

Gender equality is not only a fundamental human right, but a necessary foundation for a peaceful, prosperous and sustainable world. https://sdgs.un.org/goals/goal5

6: Clean Water and Sanitation

Clean, accessible water for all is an essential part of the world we want to live in. https://sdgs.un.org/goals/goal6

7: Affordable and Clean Energy

Energy is central to nearly every major challenge and opportunity. https://sdgs.un.org/goals/goal7

8: Decent Work and Economic Growth

Sustainable economic growth will require societies to create the conditions that allow people to have quality jobs. https://sdgs.un.org/goals/goal8

9: Industry, Innovation, and Infrastructure

Investments in infrastructure are crucial to achieving sustainable development. https://sdgs.un.org/goals/goal9

10: Reduced Inequalities

To reduce inequalities, policies should be universal in principle, paying attention to the needs of disadvantaged and marginalized populations. https://sdgs.un.org/goals/goal11

11: Sustainable Cities and Communities

There needs to be a future in which cities provide opportunities for all, with access to basic services, energy, housing, transportation and more. https://sdgs.un.org/goals/goal11

12: Responsible Consumption and Production

Responsible Production and Consumption https://sdgs.un.org/goals/goal12

13: Climate Action

Climate change is a global challenge that affects everyone, everywhere. https://sdgs.un.org/goals/goal13

14: Life Below Water

Careful management of this essential global resource is a key feature of a sustainable future. https://sdgs.un.org/goals/goal14

15: Life on Land

Sustainably manage forests, combat desertification, halt and reverse land degradation, halt biodiversity loss. https://sdgs.un.org/goals/goal15

16: Peace, Justice and Strong Institutions

Access to justice for all, and building effective, accountable institutions at all levels. https://sdgs.un.org/goals/goal16

17: Partnerships

Revitalize the global partnership for sustainable development. https://sdgs.un.org/goals/goal17

6
Conservation of Biological Diversity

1992 The Convention on Biological Diversity

Convention on
Biological Diversity

The Convention on Biological Diversity (CBD) is the foremost international legal instrument to address the loss of biological diversity and ecosystem services. It is one of three Rio Conventions arising from the 1992 UN Conference on Environment and Development (UNCED).

The three objectives of the CBD are:

1. The conservation of biological diversity
2. The sustainable use of the components of biodiversity and
3. The fair and equitable sharing of the benefits arising out of the utilization of genetic resources

As of 2016, all UN member states (a total of 196 countries and the European Union) have ratified the CBD, except the United States and the Holy See.

Conceived as a practical tool for translating the principles of Agenda 21 into reality, the Convention recognizes that biological diversity is about more than plants, animals and microorganisms and their ecosystems – it is about people and our need for food security, medicines, fresh air and water, shelter, and a clean and healthy environment in which to live.

The Convention seeks to address all threats to biodiversity and ecosystem services, including threats from climate change, through scientific assessments, the development of tools, incentives and processes, the transfer of technologies and good practices and the full and active involvement of relevant stakeholders including indigenous and local communities, youth, NGOs, women and the business community.

The CBD has 42 legally binding articles as well as two supplementary protocols: the Cartagena Protocol on Biosafety and the Nagoya Protocol on Access to Genetic Resources and the Fair and Equitable Sharing of Benefits Arising from their Utilization. Both protocols are synthesized in the next pages.

2000 The Cartagena Protocol on Biosafety

The *Cartagena Protocol on Biosafety to the Convention on Biological Diversity* is an international agreement which aims to ensure the safe handling, transport and use of living modified organisms (LMOs) resulting from modern biotechnology that may have adverse effects on biological diversity, taking also into account risks to human health. It was adopted on 29 January 2000 in Montréal and entered into force on 11 September 2003. https://youtu.be/ROY-K-a2NcQ

2010 The Nagoya Biodiversity Summit

A new era of "Living in harmony with Nature" was born at the Nagoya Biodiversity Summit, which took place in Nagoya, Aichi Prefecture, Japan on 29 October 2010, during the International Year of Biodiversity.

Preparing the Summit, Japan government set the theme of the meetings to symbolize what they aimed, reflected into the logo of COP10: "Life in harmony, in to the future." It was designed with "origami" (Japanese traditional paper folding) in the shape of various animals and plants, allocated in the surrounding circle of an adult and child, which they hope will capture the concept behind the slogan.

To materialize what this theme indicated, the government of Japan submitted a proposal in January and led international discussions. They proposed setting "living in harmony with nature" as the "vision" of a new plan, which received wide support. In addition, they proposed setting specific targets that encourage concrete actions: The Aichi Targets.

In addition, Japan government proposed a "decade on biodiversity" and advocated the "Satoyama Initiative". as one approach to realizing "living in harmony with nature." In Japanese *Satoyama* refers to managed woodlands or grasslands (*yama*) adjacent to villages (*sato*). Japan's *Satoyama* is one example of the natural environment that the

Initiative aims to maintain. It provides specific ecosystems and is closely associated with local tradition and culture, enabling local communities to fully benefit from the ecosystems through such activities as agriculture and forestry.

Satoyama

Aichi Prefecture government
Nagoya City government

During the Summit which gathered over 7,000 delegates, historic decisions concerning the challenges of the continued loss of biodiversity compounded by climate change were adopted:

• The Nagoya Protocol on Access and Benefits-Sharing (ABS) and the Fair and Equitable Sharing of Benefits arising from the utilization of genetic resources

• The Strategic Plan for Biodiversity 2010-2020 and the Aichi Biodiversity Targets **"Living in Harmony with Nature"**

• The Strategy for Resource Mobilization

The Japan Biodiversity Fund (JBF) and The Aichi Biodiversity Targets Task Force (ABTTF) also were established.

Nagoya Protocol on Access and Benefit-Sharing

The *Nagoya Protocol on Access to Genetic Resources and the Fair and Equitable Sharing of Benefits Arising from their Utilization (ABS) to the Convention on Biological Diversity* is a supplementary agreement to the Convention on Biological Diversity. It provides a transparent legal framework for the effective implementation of one of the three objectives of the CBD: the fair and equitable sharing of benefits arising out of the utilization of genetic resources. thereby contributing to the conservation and sustainable use of biodiversity. https:// youtu.be/Iltjhz6iyoA

The Nagoya Protocol on ABS was adopted on 29 October 2010 in Nagoya, Japan and entered into force on 12 October 2014, 90 days after the deposit of the fiftieth instrument of ratification.

The Strategic Plan of the Convention on Biological Diversity 2011-2020 and the Aichi Target "Living in Harmony with Nature"

The Strategic Plan for Biodiversity 2011-2020 was a ten year framework for action by all countries and stakeholders to save biodiversity and enhance its benefits for people.

To implement the Strategic Plan for Biodiversity 2011-2020, Parties were:
• reviewing, and as appropriate, updating and revising their national biodiversity strategies and action plans (NBSAPs) in line with the Strategic Plan for Biodiversity 2011-2020; •
• developing national targets, using the Strategic Plan and its Aichi Biodiversity Targets as a flexible framework,
• integrating these national targets into the updated NBSAPs.

The Aichi Targets

The Aichi Targets included 20 headline targets, organized under five strategic goals, that addressed the underlying causes of biodiversity loss, reduced the pressures on biodiversity, safeguarded biodiversity at all levels, enhanced the benefits provided by biodiversity, and provided for capacity-building.

The Aichi Biodiversity Targets

Strategic Goal A: Address the underlying causes of biodiversity loss by mainstreaming biodiversity across government and society

By 2020, at the latest people are aware of the values of biodiversity and the steps they can take to conserve and use it sustainably.

By 2020, at the latest biodiversity values have been integrated into national and local development and poverty reduction strategies and planning processes and are being incorporated into national accounting, as appropriate, and reporting systems.

By 2020, at the latest incentives, including subsidies, harmful to biodiversity are eliminated, phased out or reformed in order to minimise or avoid negative impacts, and positive incentives for the conservation and sustainable use of biodiversity are developed and applied, consistent and in harmony with the Convention and other relevant international obligations, taking into account national socio economic conditions.

By 2020, at the latest Governments, business and stakeholders at all levels have taken steps to achieve or have implemented plans for sustainable production and consumption and have kept the impacts of use of natural resources well within safe ecological limits.

By 2020 all fish and invertebrate stocks and aquatic plants are managed and harvested sustainably, legally and applying ecosystem based approaches, so that overfishing is avoided, recovery plans and measures are in place for all depleted species, fisheries have no significant adverse impacts on threatened species and vulnerable ecosystems and the impacts of fisheries on stocks, species and ecosystems are within safe ecological limits.

By 2020 areas under agriculture, aquaculture and forestry are managed sustainably, ensuring conservation of biodiversity.

By 2020, pollution, including from excess nutrients, has been brought to levels that are not detrimental to ecosystem function and biodiversity.

By 2020, invasive alien species and pathways are identified and prioritized, priority species are controlled or eradicated, and measures are in place to manage pathways to prevent their introduction and establishment.

By 2015, the multiple anthropogenic pressures on coral reefs, and other vulnerable ecosystems impacted by climate change or ocean acidification are minimized, so as to maintain their integrity and functioning

Strategic Goal C: Reduce the direct pressures on biodiversity and promote sustainable use

By 2020, the rate of loss of all natural habitats, including forests, is at least halved and where feasible brought close to zero, and degradation and fragmentation is significantly reduced.

Strategic Goal C: Improve the status of biodiversity by safeguarding ecosystems, species and genetic diversity

By 2020, at least 17 per cent of terrestrial and inland water, and 10 per cent of coastal and marine areas, especially areas of particular importance for biodiversity and ecosystem services, are conserved through effectively and equitably managed, ecologically representative and well connected systems

Special commitments were made to accomplish the following

51

- :At least halve, and where feasible bring close to zero, the rate of loss of natural habitats including forests (Target) 5
- Minimize pressures on coral reefs (Target 10)

- Establish a target of 17 per cent of terrestrial and inland water areas and 10 per cent of marine and coastal areas (Target 11)
- Restore at least 15 percent of degraded ecosystems, thereby contributing to climate change mitigation (Target 15)

Following COP10, 167 countries (Parties) developed, adopted

and updated their own National Biodiversity Strategy and Action Plan (NBSAP), taking into account the Strategic Plan for Biodiversity (2011-2020).

United Nations Decade on Biodiversity.

At the initiative of Japan, the COP10 recommended to the UN General Assembly to declared the period 2011-2020 to declare the period the United Nations Decade on Biodiversity. On December 2010, it was declared with a view to contributing to the implementation of the Strategic Plan for Biodiversity 2011-2020".

The Strategy for Resource Mobilization

• Representatives of 34 bilateral and multilateral donor agencies agreed to translate the plan into their respective development cooperation priorities.

• A Multi-Year Plan of Action on South-South Cooperation on Biodiversity for Development was adopted by the 131 member countries of the Group of 77.

• China was welcomed as an important instrument in the service of the new vision. The Prime Minister of Japan, Mr. Naoto Kan, pledged 2 billion US dollars. Additional financial resources were announced by France, the European Union, and Norway.

• Some 110 million US dollars were mobilized in support of projects under the CBD LifeWeb Initiative aimed at enhancing the protected-area agenda.

Japan Biodiversity Fund

The Japan Biodiversity Fund (JBF) was established by the Government of Japan when it assumed the COP Presidency during the tenth meeting of the Conference of the Parties (COP10), held in Nagoya, Aichi Prefecture, Japan in October 2010.The goals of the JBF are to support developing country Parties to:

1. Implement the Strategic Plan for Biodiversity 2011-2020 and its Aichi Biodiversity Targets;
2. Revise their National Biodiversity Strategy and Action Plans (NBSAPs), in the framework of the Strategic Plan; and
3. Strengthen their capacity to implement the Convention.

The Aichi Biodiversity Targets Task Force

The Aichi Biodiversity Targets Task Force (ABTTF) was established to provide a platform for agencies and organizations to coordinate their activities in support of implementation of the Strategic Plan for Biodiversity 2011-2020 and its Aichi Biodiversity Targets at global and national levels during the United Nations Decade on Biodiversity. The agencies and organizations were:

2022 The Kunming-Montreal Global Biodiversity Framework (KMGBF)

©Julian Haber

From December 7th to 19th 2022, the Second Conference of the UN Biodiversity Conference (CBD-COP 15) was held in Montréal. Delegates from 188 governments agreed on a landmark deal to guide global action to protect nature and restore ecosystems: The Kunming-Montreal Global Biodiversity Framework (GBF).

The framework includes four long-term comprehensive global goals (2050 Vision for Biodiversity), as well as 23 targets to be achieved by 2030.

The four goals are summarized in:

- Restore and conserve nature and biodiversity by stopping the mass extinction of threatened species
- The sustainable use of biodiversity and nature for the benefit of current and future generations
- The fair and equitable distribution of monetary and non-monetary benefits from the utilization of genetic resources
- Provide adequate means of implementation, including financial resources, capacity building, scientific and technological cooperation

The 23 targets take into account national circumstances, priorities and socioeconomic conditions to: reduce threats to biodiversity; meeting people's needs through sustainable use and benefit sharing, tools and solutions for implementation and integration

© Environment and Climate Change Canada

Kunming-Montreal Global Biodiversity Framework

Reduce threats to biodiversity

1. Plan and Manage all Areas To Reduce Biodiversity Loss
Managing land and sea use change effectively, to reduce the loss of areas with high biodiversity importance to close to zero by 2030, while respecting the rights of indigenous peoples and local communities.

2.Restore 30% of all of degraded terrestrial, inland water, and coastal and marine ecosystems by 2030

3. Conserve 30% of Land, Waters and Seas. Ensure effective conservation and management of 30% of terrestrial,

inland water, and coastal and marine areas by 2030, respecting the rights of indigenous peoples and local communities, including those relating to their traditional territories.
.

4. Halt Species Extinction, Protect Genetic Diversity, and Manage Human-Wildlife Conflicts. Halt human-induced extinctions and maintain and restore genetic diversity within and among populations of native, wild, and domesticated species.

5. Ensure Sustainable, Safe and Legal Harvesting and Trade of Wild Species. Ensure sustainable use, harvesting, and trade of wild species in a safe, sustainable, and legal manner, while respecting and protecting sustainable customary use by indigenous peoples and communities.

6. Reduce the Introduction of Invasive Alien Species by 50% and Minimize Their Impact. Mitigate or eliminate the impacts of invasive alien species and reduce the rates of establishment of invasive species by 50% by 2030.

7. Reduce Pollution to Levels That Are Not Harmful to Biodiversity. Reduce pollution risks and impacts from all sources by 2030, reducing the overall risk from pesticides by half as well as reducing or eliminating plastic pollution.

8.Minimize the Impacts of Climate Change on Biodiversity and Build Resilience Minimize the impacts of climate change and ocean acidification on biodiversity via mitigation, adaptation, and disaster risk reduction, among other things through nature-based solutions.,

Meeting people's needs through sustainable use and benefit sharing

9.Manage Wild Species Sustainably To Benefit People Ensure sustainable use and management of wild species, while protecting customary use by local communities and Indigenous peoples.

10.Enhance Biodiversity and Sustainability in Agriculture, Aquaculture, Fisheries, and Forestry. Manage areas under agriculture, aquaculture, fisheries, and forestry sustainably, among other things, by substantially increasing the use of biodiversity-friendly practices, such as sustainable intensification approaches, agro-ecological approaches.

11. Restore, Maintain and Enhance Nature's Contributions to People. Restore and enhance ecosystem function through nature-based solutions and ecosystem-based approaches, including ecosystem functions and services, such as air, water and climate regulation, soil health, pollination and disease risk reduction, as well as protection from natural hazards and disasters , through nature-based solutions.

12. Enhance Green Spaces and Urban Planning for Human Well-Being and Biodiversity, as well as access to them and the benefits derived from them, in a sustainable manner and guarantee urban planning that takes into account biological diversity, improving the health and well-being of human beings and their connection with nature.

13. Increase the Sharing of Benefits From Genetic Resources, Digital Sequence Information and Traditional Knowledge Share the benefits arising from the use of genetic resources fairly and equitably.

Tools and solutions for implementation and mainstreaming

14. Integrate Biodiversity in Decision-Making at Every Level. Integrate biodiversity into policies and development across all sectors, including aligning public and private activities.

15. Businesses Assess, Disclose and Reduce Biodiversity-Related Risks and Negative Impacts. Provide policy measure to enable businesses to monitor, assess, and disclose their impacts on biodiversity.
.

16. Enable Sustainable Consumption Choices To Reduce Waste and Overconsumption. Encourage sustainable consumption, including by reducing food waste by half by 2030.

17. Strengthen Biosafety and Distribute the Benefits of Biotechnology. Strengthen capacity for biosafety measures and ensure benefits sharing from biotechnology

18. Reduce Harmful Incentives by at Least $500 Billion per Year, and Scale Up Positive Incentives for Biodiversity. Identify and eliminate harmful subsidies in a just way, reducing them by $500 billion by 2030

19. Mobilize $200 Billion per Year for Biodiversity From all Sources, Including $30 Billion, Through International Financing; stimulating innovative schemes, such as payments for ecosystem services, green bonds; reinforcing the role of collective actions, including those of indigenous peoples and local communities, actions focused on Mother Earth., and promote the development of and access to South-South, North-South and triangular scientific and technical cooperation and innovation for biodiversity in a manner commensurate with the level of ambition of the Framework's objectives and targets.

20. Strengthen Capacity-Building, Technology Transfer, and Scientific and Technical Cooperation for Biodiversity and promote the development of and access to South-South, North-South and triangular scientific and technical cooperation and innovation for biodiversity in a manner commensurate with the level of ambition of the Framework's objectives and targets.

21. Ensure That Knowledge Is Available and Accessible To Guide Biodiversity Action. Promote integrated and participatory management, including the use of traditional knowledge, innovations, practices, and technologies of indigenous peoples and local communities only with their free, prior and informed consent, in accordance with national legislation.

22. Ensure Participation in Decision-Making and Access to Justice and Information Related to Biodiversity, for all and representation of indigenous peoples and local communities, respecting their cultures and rights over lands, territories, resources and traditional knowledge. , as well as women and girls, children and youth and people with disabilities, and guarantee the full protection of defenders of human rights related to the environment.

23. Ensure Gender Equality and a Gender-Responsive Approach for Biodiversity Action, regarding rights and access to lands and natural resources and their participation and leadership at all levels of action, participation, policy formulation and decision-making related to biodiversity.

Summarizing the special commitments:

- Restoration of 30% of global marine and terrestrial ecosystems (Goal 1)
- Effective management of 30% of oceans, lands and coastal zones (Target 2)
- Reducing pollution from nutrients, pesticides, chemicals and plastic pollution (Goal 7)
- Increase in green and blue spaces in urban areas (Goal 12)
- Recognition and respect for the rights of indigenous peoples and local communities (Goals 1, 3)
- Respect, protection and promotion of the sustainable customary use of wild species (Goal 5, 9)
- Increasing their participation in the benefits derived from the use of genetic resources and traditional knowledge (Goal 13)
- The guarantee of free consent, their participation and representation in decision-making, their access to justice and information related to biodiversity (Goals 21, 22)

- Guarantee the participation and representation of women and girls, children and youth and people with disabilities, and guarantee the full protection of defenders of human rights related to the environment (Goal 22)
- The guarantee of gender equality, their participation and leadership at all levels of action, participation, policy formulation and decision-making related to biodiversity (Goal 23)

The Kunming Biodiversity Fund

In October 2021, China had announced the initiative to establish the Kunming Biodiversity Fund. During the first part of the 15th meeting of (COP15), held in Kunming. China took the lead by investing 1.5 billion yuan ($233 million)

During the second part of the 15th meeting (COP15), held in Montréal, the Kunming Biodiversity Fund was adopted.

2024 Cali, Colombia COP16

The "People's COP" was held in Cali, Colombia from October 21st to November 2nd, 2024. With the vibrant backdrop of salsa music and local culture, this event brought together more than 700,000 participants who passed through the green zone, a record for any CBD COP. Cali Fund was established, expecting to raise up to $1 billion yearly for conserving biodiversity.

.
H.E. Susana Muhamad, Minister of Environment and Sustainable Development and COP 16 President wrote: "All the decisions taken in Cali benefit the protection of biodiversity and recognize the work of indigenous peoples and local communities, afrodescendent communities and campesinos as guardians and protectors of biodiversity...The World Coalition for Peace with Nature is our great legacy to the world…" https://www.cbd.int/article/agreement-reached-cop-16

7
Climate Change

Scientific awareness

In 1986 Swedish Svante Arrhenius was the first Scientists that awareness us, that burning fossil was pumping CO2 levels so significant that could cause global warming. No one paid attention to his publication. However in 1930's measurements showed that average temperatures of US and Northern Atlantic was increasing without knowing exactly the reason.

By **1938 Guy Stewart Callendar** a British engineer and inventor started collecting data on concentration and properties of the atmospheric gases, on the rainfalls and temperatures across the globe, on the role of the ocean currents and use of fossil fuels. As a result, he produced the first accurate mathematical model simulating climate behavior. Members of The Royal Meteorological Society ignored it saying that a person with no relevant PhD could not be right on such a complex issue. But Callendar never gave up on theory and kept working on it. Callendar's study raised quite a lot of curiosity among the scientific community. In the1950's he publicly stated that climate change is really happening.

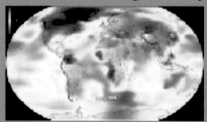

On **June 23, 1988 James Hansen** one of the leading NASA scientists gave testimony to the US Senate committee on energy and national resources that, according to NASA computer simulations, climate change is already large enough to cause extreme weather events and with 99% certainty it is caused by human actions. His statement made headlines around the world. A real discussion started between public scientists and politicians; as one of the measures, United Nations established:The **Intergovernmental Panel on Climate Change**

1992 UN Framework Convention on Climate Change

As mentioned in Chapter 5, at the Rio Earth Summit in June 1992, the United Nations Framework Convention on Climate Change (UNFCCC) was signed. The Convention entered into force on March 21, 1994. Today, it has almost universal adherence. The 198 countries.

Its goal is to stabilize greenhouse gas concentrations "at a level that would prevent dangerous anthropogenic (human-induced) interference with the climate system."

It states that "that level should be reached within a sufficient timeframe to allow ecosystems to adapt naturally to climate change, ensure that food production is not threatened, and allow economic development to proceed in a sustainable manner."

It was remarkable at that time since at that time, there was little scientific evidence of the problem that was being experienced
The Convention borrowed an important line from one of the most successful multilateral environmental treaties in history, the

1997 Montreal Protocol, compelling member states to act in the interests of human security in the face of scientific uncertainty.

1997 The Kyoto Protocol, Japan

The Kyoto Protocol was approved on December 11, 1997. Due to a complex ratification process, it entered into force on February 16, 2005.

The Kyoto Protocol

• Operationalizes the United Nations Framework Convention on Climate Change by committing industrialized countries and economies in transition to limit and reduce greenhouse gases (GHG) emissions in accordance with agreed individual targets. In

• Sets binding emission reduction targets for 37 industrialized countries and economies in transition and the European Union. Overall these targets add up to an average 5 per cent emission reduction compared to 1990 levels over the five year period 2008–2012

• Established a rigorous monitoring, review and verification system, as well as a compliance system to ensure transparency and hold Parties to account. The UN Climate Change Secretariat, based in Bonn, Germany, kept an international transaction log to verify that transactions were consistent with the rules of the Protocol.

In 2001,The Adaptation Fund was established to finance adaptation projects and programs in developing countries that are Parties to the Kyoto Protocol.

In Doha, in 2012, the Kyoto Protocol was amended in Doha, Qatar during the COP18 on Climate Change

The Doha Amendment to the Kyoto Protocol included:

• New responsibilities for the Parties to the Kyoto Protocol, who agreed to new commitments for a second period (2013-2020)

- A revised list of GHGs that Parties should report on in the second commitment period

- In 2015, the Kyoto Protocol was replaced by the Paris Agreement.

2015 Paris Agreement

©Arnaud BouissouMEDDE

To tackle climate change and its negative impacts, two months after the achievement of SDGs, world leaders at the UN Climate Change Conference (COP21) in Paris reached a breakthrough on 12 December 2015: the historic Paris Agreement. The Agreement is a legally binding international treaty. It entered into force on 4 November 2016

There were 36,000 participants, nearly 23,100 government officials, 9,400 representatives from UN bodies and agencies, intergovernmental organizations and civil society organizations, and 3,700 members of the media.

Governments agreed that mobilizing stronger and more ambitious climate action was urgently required to achieve the goals of the Paris Agreement. To connect the work of governments with the many voluntary and collaborative actions taken by cities, regions, businesses and investors, nations decided to appoint two high-level Champions. In 2016, H.E. Mrs. Laurence Tubiana was designated as first High-Level Champion.

The Agreement set long-term goals to guide all nations:

Substantially reduce global greenhouse gas emissions to limit the global temperature increase in this century to 2 degrees Celsius while pursuing efforts to limit the increase even further to 1.5 degrees review countries' commitments every five years provide financing to developing countries to mitigate climate change, strengthen resilience and enhance abilities to adapt to climate impacts.

Also, the Paris Agreement:

• Included commitments from all countries to reduce their emissions and work together to adapt to the impacts of climate change, and calls on countries to strengthen their commitments over time.

• Marked the beginning of a shift towards a net-zero emissions world.

• Provided a pathway for developed nations to assist developing nations in their climate mitigation and adaptation efforts while creating a framework for the transparent monitoring and reporting of countries' climate goals.

Implementation of the Agreement is essential for the achievement of the Sustainable Development Goals.

2016 COP 22 UNFCCC Marrakech

From November 7 to 8, 2016, in Marrakech, Morocco, delegates pushed forward with the freshly-minted Paris Agreement, setting 2018 as their deadline for completing the nuts-and-bolts decisions needed to fully implement the agreement.Negotiators focused on developing rules for implementing the agreement, including the reporting and review of countries' climate efforts; a

© Ximena Navarro

new five-year cycle to assess progress and update parties' contributions; and the use of market-based approaches.

The Marrakech conference capped an extraordinary year of global progress on climate change: the Paris Agreement's swift entry into force, a new agreement to cap emissions from international aviation, and a deal to phase down powerful climate pollutants known as HFCs. https://www.c2es.org/content/cop-22-marrakech/.

During the conference, It was also launched the Marrakech Partnership for Global Climate Action which will be summarized in the following page.

2016 The Marrakech Partnership for Global Climate Action

(MP-GCA), provided a framework to enhanced and accelerated global climate action among Parties and non-Party stakeholders (NPS) of international and regional initiatives and coalitions of cities, regions, businesses, investors, and civil society. It focused on immediate climate action that supported the implementation of the Paris Agreement.

The following years, not much work was done. However, in preparation and after COP26, new campaigns started:

The Marrakech Partnership, together with the High Level Champions, have been rallying NPS three global campaigns:

1..Race to Zero
2..Race to Resilience
3..Glasgow Financial Alliance for Net Zero (GFANZ)

There has been focus on driving system transformations that are needed to stay within the 1.5-degree limit.

2020 Race to Zero Campaign

Led by the High-Level Champions, Race to Zero global campaign mobilized actors outside of national governments to join the Climate Ambition Alliance, launched at the UNSG's Climate Action Summit 2019 by the President of Chile, Sebastián Piñera.

Race to Zero is a rallying non-state actors including companies, cities, regions, financial, educational, and healthcare institutions to take rigorous and immediate action to halve global emissions by 2030 and deliver a healthier, fairer, net zero world.

Since June 2020, over 13,000 members have joined the campaign and are committed to the same overarching goal: reducing emissions across all scopes swiftly and fairly in line with the Paris Agreement with transparent action plans and robust near-term targets. All members meet robust science-aligned criteria, which was clarified and strengthened through an extensive consultation process in June 2022. Partner initiatives are responsible for helping to bring members to the starting line to credibly race to zero emissions.

It mobilizes a coalition of leading net-zero initiatives, representing 11,309 non-State actors including 8,307 companies, 595 financial institutions, 1,136 cities, 52 states and regions, 1,125 educational institutions and 65 healthcare institutions (as of September 2022). These 'real economy' actors join the largest-ever alliance committed to achieving net zero carbon emissions by 2050 at latest.

2021 Race to Resilience Campaign

 The High Level Climate Champions Race to Resilience — the sibling campaign to Race To Zero — was launched at the Climate Adaptation Summit on January 25, 2021 by Alok Sharma, COP26 President designate. The campaign set out to catalyze a step-change in global ambition for climate resilience putting people and nature first in pursuit of a resilient world where we don't just survive climate shocks and stresses but thrive in spite of them.

Led by the High-Level Climate Champions for Climate Action – Nigel Topping and Gonzalo Muñoz – Race to Resilience aims:

By 2030, to catalyze action by non-state actors that builds the resilience of 4 billion people from vulnerable groups and communities to climate risks

Through a partnership of initiatives, the campaign will focus on helping frontline communities to build resilience and adapt to impacts of climate change, such as extreme heat, drought, flooding and sea-level rise.

- Urban: Transform urban slums into healthy, clean and safe cities
- Rural: Equip smallholder farmers to adapt and thrive
- Coastal: Protect homes and businesses against climate shocks

The Race to Resilience has 28 Partners, representing over 2,000 organizations, delivering action in over 100 countries.

The Glasgow Financial Alliance for Net Zero (GFANZ) was launched in April 2021 by UN Special Envoy on Climate Action and Finance Mark Carney and the COP26 presidency, in partnership with the UNFCCC Race to Zero campaign, to coordinate efforts across all sectors of the financial system to accelerate the transition to a net-zero global economy.

It is the world's largest coalition of financial institutions committed to transitioning the global economy to net-zero greenhouse gas emissions by 2050 helping to achieve the objectives of the Paris Agreement.

GFANZ brings together independent, sector-specific Alliances to tackle net-zero transition challenges and connects the financial community to the Race to Zero campaign, climate scientists and experts, and civil society. The members of each Alliance operate in a diverse range of economies and financial systems spanning the developed, emerging and developing world. It counts with 500 members firms around 50 countries.

2021 COP26 Together for our planet Glasgow UK

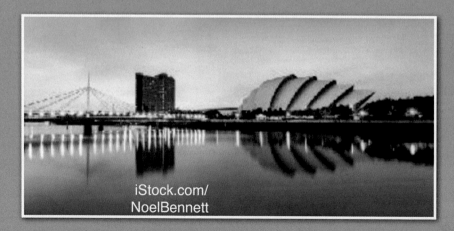

iStock.com/
NoelBennett

The UN Climate Change Conference in Glasgow (COP26) brought together 120 world leaders and over 40,000 registered participants, including 22,274 party delegates, 14.124 observers and 3.886 media representatives.

From 31 October to 13 November 2021, the world was riveted on all facets of climate change, the science, the solutions, the political will to act, and clear indications of action.

The outcome of COP26 was the Glasgow Climate Pact. It was the fruit of intense negotiations among almost 200 countries over the two weeks, strenuous formal and informal work over many months, and constant engagement both in-person and virtually for nearly two years. "The approved texts are a compromise," said UN Secretary-General António Guterres. "They reflect the interests, the conditions, the contradictions and the state of political will in the world today. They take important steps, but unfortunately the collective political will was not enough to overcome some deep contradictions."

2021 The Breakthrough Agenda

At COP26 in November 2021, 45 world leaders, whose governments collectively represent over 70% of global GDP, launched the Breakthrough Agenda, aiming at strengthening international collaboration on decarbonizing high-emitting sectors (Transport, Power, Hydrogen, Steel, and Agriculture) and making clean technologies and sustainable solutions the most affordable, accessible and attractive option in all regions by 2030.

Under this Agenda, leaders agreed to review progress annually and explore priority international actions needed to accelerate the Breakthroughs, informed by an annual independent expert report from the International Energy Agency (IEA), International Renewable Energy Agency (IRENA), and UN High-Level Champions.

The inaugural Breakthrough Agenda Report 2022 was published in September 2022.

2022 COP27 Sharm el-Sheikh Egypt

©UN Kiara Worth

From 6 to 20 November, COP27 held high-level and side events, key negotiations, and press conferences, hosting more than 100 Heads of State and Governments, over 35,000 participants and numerous pavilions showcasing climate action around the world and across different sectors.

At COP27, two youth activists Elizabeth Wathuti and Archana Soreng and the winner of the #MyClimateAction contest Ewi Stephanie Lamma demanded urgent action from world leaders amid the worsening climate crisis.

After days of intense negotiations, countries reached agreement on establishing a fund to compensate vulnerable nations for 'loss and damage' from climate-induced disasters.

COP27 concluded with a historic decision to establish and operationalize a loss and damage fund. "Together, let's not relent in the fight for climate justice and climate ambition," said the UN Secretary-General in his closing messaging. "We can and must win this battle for our lives."

Also, at COP 27 were launched:

1. The Sharm el Sheikh Adaptation Agenda (SAA)
2. The Sustainable Urban Resilience for the next Generation (SURGe)

On 8 November 2022, the COP27 Presidency, in partnership with the High-Level Champions, launched the Sharm el Sheikh Adaptation Agenda (SAA) The agenda aims to focus global action on 30 adaptation targets needed to close the gap and create a resilience world by 2023. https://www.swedev.dev/cop27-launch-of-the-sharm-el-sheikh-adaptation-agenda/

"The 30 Adaptation Outcomes include urgent global 2030 targets related to:

• Transitioning to climate resilient, sustainable agriculture that can increase yields by 17% and reduce farm level greenhouse gas (GHG) emissions by 21%, without expanding agricultural frontiers, and while improving livelihoods including of smallholder farmers.

• Protecting and restoring an estimated 400 million hectares in critical areas (land and freshwater ecosystems) supporting indigenous and local communities with use of nature-based solutions to improve water security and livelihoods and to transform 2 billion hectares of land into sustainable management

• Protecting 3 billion people by installing smart and early warning systems

• Investing USD 4 billion to secure the future of 15 million hectares of mangroves through collective action to halt loss, restore, double protection and ensure sustainable finance for all existing mangroves.

• Expanding access to clean cooking for 2.4 billion people through at least USD 10 billion/year in innovative finance

• Mobilizing USD 140 to USD 300 billion needed across both public and private sources for adaptation and resilience and spur 2,000 of the world's largest companies to integrate physical climate risk and develop actionable adaptation plans"

COP27 Sustainable Urban Resilience for the next Generation (SURGe)

Cities are at the frontline of climate change. Though cities are a big driver of planet-warming emissions, they are also engines of climate action and at the forefront of delivering solutions. That's why we need effective multi-level governance to transform cities to be healthy, sustainable, just, inclusive, low-emission and resilient urban systems for a better urban future for all.

To achieve this vision, the COP27 Presidency launched the Sustainable Urban Resilience for the Next Generation (SURGe)

Initiative – with the objective to enhance and accelerate local and urban climate action through multi-level governance, engagement, and delivery through five integrated tracks, contributing to achieving the Paris Climate Goals and Sustainable Development Goals.

The SURGe Initiative was developed in collaboration with UN-Habitat and facilitated by ICLEI and has been endorsed by 70+ global partners. SURGe was officially launched at the Urban and Housing Ministerial Session on Cities and Climate Change at COP27.

2023 COP28 Dubai

©Mahmoud Khaled

From November 30 until December, 2023, the COP28 was held in Dubai, UAE. There were registered 80,000 official participants :23,500 people from official government teams, 27,208 policy experts, academics, representatives, senior company executives from oil giants, and more than 14,000 non-governmental organizations including indigenous people, women, youth and local communities.

In a demonstration of global solidarity, negotiators from nearly 200 Parties came together in Dubai with a decision on the world's first 'global stock take to ratchet up climate action before the end of the decade – with the overarching aim to keep the global temperature limit of 1.5°C within reach."AN AGREEMENT IS ONLY AS GOOD AS ITS IMPLEMENTATION. THIS HISTORIC CONSENSUS IS ONLY THE BEGINING.
https://youtu.be/VMzKIzWdkvA?si=UeWtV3AeIGljVwMu

It was opening with the announcement of a loss and damage fund of $ 227 million was created. The fond increased up to $792 million at the end of the conference

COP28 closed with the UAE Consensus that signals the "beginning of the end" of the fossil fuel era by laying the ground for a swift, just and equitable transition, underpinned by deep emissions cuts and scaled-up finance. "Now all governments and businesses need to turn these pledges into real-economy outcomes, without delay", said UN Climate Change Executive Secretary Simon Stiell in his closing speech.

198 PARTIES HAVE UNITED BEHIND THE UAE CONSENSUS. A NEW PATH FOR THE WORLD. AN ENHANCED, BALANCED AND HISTORIC PACKAGE TO ACCELERATE CLIMATE ACTION.

At COP28, the following Declarations were also signed:

- UAE Leaders' Declaration on A Global Climate Finance Framework
- COP28 Declaration on Climate, Relief, Recovery And Peace
- Gender-responsive Just Transitions And Climate Action Partnership
- Coalition for High Ambition Multilevel Partnerships (Champ) For Climate Action
- COP28 UAE Declaration on Climate And Health
- COP28 Declaration of Intent
- Sustainable Agriculture, Resilient Food Systems, And Climate Action
- Global Cooling Pledge for COP28
- Global Renewables and Energy Efficiency Pledge
- COP28 Joint Statement on Climate, Nature And People

2023 Breakthrough Agenda

©climatechampions.unfcc.

In 2024, the United Nations High-Level Champion for Climate Change in the United Arab Emirates, COP28 Her Excellency Ms. Razan Al Mubarak and the United Nations High-Level Champion for Climate Change in Azerbaijan, for the next

COP29, Ms. Nigar Arpadarai, continued the efforts of her predecessors on climate change

The 2023 Breakthrough Agenda contemplates international collaboration between governments, regions, cities, companies, investors and civil society, to ensure that low-carbon transitions are faster, less difficult, less costly and with higher profits.

More than forty countries are committed to working together in every emitting sector to accelerate the development and implementation of clean technologies and sustainable solutions, ensuring they are affordable and accessible to all.

Some specific objectives for the sector of Nature, Land Use, are:

- Address the. Deforestation and scaling up Nature-Based Solutions (NBS)

- Guarantee the rights of indigenous and local communities, protect 45 million hectares, restore 350 million hectares of degraded lands and sustainably manage forests and other terrestrial biomes

- Pivot towards positive use of land, food and agriculture that favors Nature base Solutions

- Reduce 10 Gt (1,000,000,000 tons) of CO_2e through nature-based solutions including protecting 45 MHa (1,000,000 hectares), restoring 350 MHa (1,000,000 hectares) of land and the food system.

Some specific objectives for the Ocean and coastal areas are:

- Invest $4 billion to halt loss, restore half and double protection of 17 million hectares of mangroves

- In the ocean renewable energy sector, install at least 380 GW of marine disability, while establishing targets and enabling measures to achieve net positive biodiversity outcomes and mobilizing $10 billion in concessional financing for developing economies. development achieve this goal

- Secure the future of at least 125,000 km2 of shallow-water tropical coral reefs with an investment of at least $12 billion to support the resilience of more than 500 million people worldwide by 2023.

- Provide at least $4 billion to support aquatic food systems that contribute to healthy, regenerative ecosystems and sustain food and nutrition security for 3 million people.

COP28 Ocean Pavilion

The ocean is the largest living space on Earth and a fundamental part of our planetary climate system. But human activity, particularly in the form of greenhouse gas emissions that adversely impact the heat content, sea level, and acidity of the oceans, interferes with the ocean's ability to support marine and terrestrial life, and hinders sustainable development worldwide. The COP28 Climate Ocean Pavilion served as a dynamic learning and collaboration platform which fostered interaction between scientists and policymakers in the collective pursuit of solutions to some of the world's most pressing challenges..

At COP28 Dubai, the Ocean Pavilion's partners and associated, signed the Ocean Declaration, calling on world leaders to support and foster efforts to:

• Improve global inventory estimates and measures of progress toward the goals set out in the Paris Agreement by providing better measures of carbon fluxes through the ocean and a more comprehensive view of Earth's ocean-climate system.

• Implement robust and cooperative monitoring, reporting and verification of new and emerging ocean carbon dioxide removal strategies to ensure measurable progress toward net negative emissions while protecting critical ocean ecosystems.

• Expand observational capabilities to measure the broadest possible set of climate and biological variables essential to better understand and address the impacts of climate change on the distribution of ocean life, the health of marine ecosystems, biomass and biodiversity.

• Build capacity among island nations and developing countries and refine methodologies to take into account the contributions of natural functions of the ocean and the blue economy to climate stabilization through nationally determined contributions and national adaptation plans.
https://oceanpavilion-cop.org/dubai-ocean-declaration/

2024 COP29 Baku, Azerbaijan

COP29 was held in Baku, Azerbaijan from November 11th until November 24th, 2024. After two weeks of intensive negotiations and several years of preparatory work, it concluded with a new finance goal agreement calling on developed countries to deliver $300 billion per year to developing countries by 2035 to drastically reduce greenhouse gas emissions and protect lives and livelihoods from the worsening impacts of climate change. "I had hoped for a more ambitious outcome – on both finance and mitigation – to meet the great challenge we face," UN Secretary-General António Guterres said in his <u>statement</u> on COP29. "But this agreement provides a base on which to build."<u>https://www.un.org/en/climatechange/cop29</u>

© COP29, Baku, Azerbaijan

COP29 also reached an agreement on carbon markets to help countries better achieve their climate plans.

The Conference took a decisive step forward to elevate the voices of Indigenous Peoples and local communities in climate action, adopting the <u>Baku Workplan</u> and marked a significant milestone as dedicated spaces were created to ensure the meaningful participation of children within the Youth-led Climate Forum for the first time.

At COP29, the United Nations High-Level Champions for Climate Change, launched the <u>2024 Yearbook of Global Climate Action</u>, the Marrakech Partnership for Global Climate Action.

"So this is no time for victory laps. We need to set our sights and redouble our efforts on the road to Belem....The UN Paris Agreement is humanity's life-raft… we're taking that journey forward together." said Simon Stiell, Executive Secretary of UN Climate Change at the COP29 closing speech.
COP30 will be held in 2025 in Belem, Brazil.

COP29 Ocean Declaration

A summary of the COP29 Ocean Declaration is: The ocean is critical for achieving the climate mitigation and adaptation objectives of the 29th Conference of the UNFCCC Parties. It is the planet's largest carbon sink and currently absorbs nearly one-quarter to one-third of human-caused carbon dioxide emissions and 90% of heat generated by anthropogenic greenhouse gas emissions. For that reason, ocean-based climate solutions can offer significant opportunities to keep the crucial 1.5°C target within reach.

The global community should prioritize ocean-based actions that will support progress toward priorities shared by the climate, biodiversity, and desertification COPs, including:

• Expand international collaboration;
• Enhance public and private funding
• Build capacity and access;
• Improve awareness of the ocean's role in planetary systems
https://oceanpavilion-cop.org/baku-ocean-declaration/#signatories

Conclusions

The valuable legacy of indigenous people and local communities, passionate people, scientists, economists, world leaders knowledge, as well as the recognition of civil society, business and youth input to safe life on the planet for our children and future generations is showing progress.

Indigenous people have a deep connection with the Mother Earth and respect for all living creatures. Their knowledge is a great source of wisdom, guidance, and inspiration.

"We must protect the forests for our children, grandchildren and children yet to be born. We must protect the forests for those who can't speak for themselves such as the birds, animals, fish and trees."Qwatsinas (Hereditary Chief Edward Moody), Nuxalk Nation

IUCN, BirdLife, Nature Conservancy, WWF, Greenpeace, Conservation International, Half-Earth Project, and uncountable NGOs, including scientists, youth, and civil society are working with national and local government to attain by 2023 the GBF Goals and targets, especially:

Restore 30% of all Degraded Ecosystems
Conserve 30% of Land, Waters and Seas

IUCN, the world's largest and diverse environmental network, with their 18,000 international experts, all over the world, led by H.E. Ms. Razan Al Mubara, current UN Climate Change Co High-Level Champion for COP27 and COP28 are working tirelessly to champion Nature-based Solutions programs as key to the implementation of the SDGs and Paris Agreement:

Keep the global temperature limit of 1.5 c
Net-zero emission world.

Thanks to the international meetings' participants, a great step has been taken by the United Nations' agreements to protect and conserve life on our Blue Planet. From the first Human Environment Conference in Stockholm, Sweden in 1972, with 1,200 delegates representing 113 countries to the UNFCC UAE COP28 in Dubai, in 2023, with 80,000 official participants, where 198 Parties signed the UAE Consensus.

At Dubai, they were all together facing the global challenges and working for solutions. **"We have shown that humanity can come together to help humanity**... I hope that the spirit of partnership, inclusivity and peace that has welcomed you here in the UAE, goes with you from this place, and lives on for the good of all humanity" said the COP28 President Dr. Sultan Al Jaber at Closing Plenary.

Four main global challenges we are facing this decade: Sustainable Development, Conservation and Protection of Biodiversity, a clean, healthy, resilient, and productive ocean, and Climate Change. It is necessary to continue enhancing the collaboration among governments, scientists, economists, world leaders, civil society, business, and youth to take action to create solutions.
.
What could each of us do to protect "Mother Earth" and Live in Harmony with Nature GFB's Vision: "By 2050, biodiversity is valued, conserved, restored and wisely used, maintaining ecosystem services, sustaining a healthy planet and delivering benefits essential for all people"?

Learn from the wisdom of indigenous peoples, local communities and our ancestors about

Respect for Nature
The medicinal plants
Caring for the land, water and air

Keep the air fresh

84

Walking, scootering, bicycling, and using public transportation
Indispensable flying
Participating in virtual meetings instead of traveling
Planting trees
Encourage the use of live Christmas trees
Change our consumption habits by producing and buying only essential things
Avoiding aerosol sprays

Take care of the water that flows from the sources, through the streams and rivers to the oceans.

Rinsing immediately our cup, plates and utensils, as the Japanese clean their cup of tea
Avoiding chemicals soaps
Using traditional cleaning solutions such as lemon to remove grease (kitchen utensils will be as clean as the leaves of trees every time the rain comes)
Changing our consumption of plastic bottles, containers, and bags
Kayaking, canoeing, and sailing
Reusing again baskets and glass containers

Sustaining a healthy soil

Learning more from Indigenous people about taking care of "Mother Earth"
Sharing knowledge about medicinal plants
Seeding and planting flowers, vegetables, and herbs at home or in community gardens
Composting
Joining environmental communities, regional and national organizations

Enjoying living creatures around us

Learning about the cycle of life of each one we encounter
Admiring the butterflies
Observing the honeybees, which pollinate 84% of our food supply (with their wings flapping 230 times per second, the

bees fly about 3 times the orbit of the Earth to gather 2 pounds of honey in their life)
Blowing to the flys which come close to us and ward out them with smoke, as our ancestors did
Becoming friends with every single bird who comes to sing
Being curious about how far the   ones we see and listen to travel
Cuddling the domestic creatures
Discovering new creatures in the streams, rivers, and lakes

Learning about the living creatures far from us

The migration of the elephants, giraffes, wildebeest and caribous
The oceans where whales, sharks, rays, marine turtles, salmon, and sturgeon swim
The continents through the geese, arctic terns and tiny monarch butterflies fly, the periods and the length of their journey
The mammal's adaptation on the frozen Arctic tundra: polar bear, Arctic fox, Arctic hare, reindeer, musk ox and wolverine
The extraordinary life of the Arctic aquatic creatures: orcas, narwhals, beluga whales, walrus, seals, as well as the birds: puffins, ptarmigan, bald eagle and the Arctic terns
Discovering the Antarctic seabird: the small Arctic tern (which flies 40,000 km 25,000 miles from the Arctic), the large wandering albatross, the Antarctic shag, the snowy sheathbill, the kelp gull, the wilson's storm petrel
Admiring the diversity and life of penguins in the Antarctic
Becoming enlightened with the colossal Antarctic squid and the giant Antarctic Octopus and the tiny krill
Becoming familiar with the Antarctic seals: the Southern elephant, the Crabeater, the Antarctic Fur, the Leopard, the Ross, and the Weddell
Learning about Galapagos Blue and Red footed boobies

Communicating with friendly dolphin and powerful whales all over the oceans

« If you talk to the animals, they will talk with you, and you will know each other. If you do not…you will only know your own kind » — *Black Elk*

Benefiting from the energy of heaven and earth

Turn off lights when not needed
Use solar lamps, chargers, and generators at home
Marvel at the beauty of daily sunrise and sunset
Learn about the moon's influence on earth
Follow the movement of planets and stars at night
Be aware of happiness and peace

Remind yourself every day "What A Wonderful World" we live in and we take care of the ones to come.

https://youtu.be/auSo1MyWf8g?si=wXRvikMtGQe9XJO6«

«The earth does not belong to man; man belongs to the earth. » — *Chief Seattle*

Acronyms

ABTTF	Aichi Biodiversity Targets Task Force
ASB	Access on Benefit-Sharing
BBNJ	Biodiversity Beyond Nation Jurisdiction
CBD	Convention on Biological Diversity
CITES	Convention on International Trade on Endangered Species of Wilde Fauna and Flora
CMS	Convention Migratory Species
COP10	UNCBD Nagoya, Japan 2010
COP15	UNCBD Kunming-Montreal 2022
COP21	UNFCCC Paris Agreement 2015
COP22	UNFCCC Marrakech 2016
COP26	UNFCCC Glasgow 2021
COP27	UNFCCC Sharm el-Sheikh 2022
COP28	UNFCCC Dubai 2023
ES	Ecosystem services
FAO	Food and Agriculture Organization
GBIF	Global Biodiversity Information
GEF	Global Environment Facility
GFANZ	Glasgow Financial Alliance for Net Zero
GOOS	Global Ocean Observation System
ICBP	International Council for Bird Protection
IOC	Intergovernmental Oceanographic Commission
IODE	International Oceanographic Data and Information Exchange

IOI	International Ocean Institute
IPBES	Intergovernmental Science-Policy Platform on Biodiversity and Ecosystem Services
IPLC	Indigenous People and Local Communities
IPPC	International Plant Protection Convention
IUCN	International Union for Conservation of Nature
IWC	International Whaling Commission
JBF	Japan Biodiversity Fund
KMGBF	Kunming-Montreal Global Biodiversity Framework
LDC	Least Developed Country
LMO	Living Modified Organisms
NBSAP	National Biodiversity Strategy and Action Plan
OBIS	Ocean Biodiversity Information System
OECD	Organization for Economic Cooperation and Development
OL	Ocean Literacy
SDGs	Sustainable Development Goals
SIDS	Small Islands Developing States
SURGe	Sustainable Urban Resilience for the next Generation
UN	United Nations
UNCCD	United Nations Convention to Combat Desertification
UNCLOS I	United Nations Conference on the Law of the Sea

UNCLOS	United Nations Convention on the Law of the Sea
UNDP	United Nations Development Programme
UNESCO	United Nations Educational, Scientific and Cultural Organization
IOC	Intergovernmental Oceanographic Commission
IODE	International Oceanographic Data and Information Exchange
IOI	International Ocean Institute
IPBES	Intergovernmental Science-Policy Platform on Biodiversity and Ecosystem Services
IPLC	Indigenous People and Local Communities
IPPC	International Plant Protection Convention
IUCN	International Union for Conservation of Nature
IWC	International Whaling Commission
JBF	Japan Biodiversity Fund
KMGBF	Kunming-Montreal Global Biodiversity Framework
LDC	Least Developed Country
LMO	Living Modified Organisms
NBSAP	National Biodiversity Strategy and Action Plan
OBIS	Ocean Biodiversity Information System
OECD	Organization for Economic Cooperation and Development
OL	Ocean Literacy
SDGs	Sustainable Development Goals
SIDS	Small Islands Developing States

SURGe	Sustainable Urban Resilience for the next Generation
UN	United Nations
UNCCD	United Nations Convention to Combat Desertification
UNCLOS I	United Nations Conference on the Law of the Sea
UNCLOS	United Nations Convention on the Law of the Sea
UNDP	United Nations Development Program
UNESCO	United Nations Educational, Scientific and Cultural Organization

Glossary

Acceptance or Approval
The instruments of "acceptance" or "approval" of a treaty have the same legal effect as ratification and consequently express the consent of a state to be bound by a treaty. It is used when at a national level, constitutional law does not require the treaty to be ratified by the head of state

Accession
 "Accession" is the act whereby a state accepts the offer or the opportunity to become a party to a treaty already negotiated and signed by other states. It has the same legal effect as ratification. Accession usually occurs after the treaty has entered into force

Adoption
"Adoption" is the formal act by which the form and content of a proposed treaty text is established

Agreement
An agreement is a manifestation of mutual assent by two or more persons to one another

Biodiversity
Biodiversity is a term that represents the total variety of total life on earth: thousands of differences wild habitats, millions of different species, billions of different individuals, and a trillions of different characteristics they all have. The more biodiversity, the more secure all life on earth is, including ourselves

Conference of the Parties (COP)
The COP is the supreme decision-making body of a Convention, consisting of all governments and regional economic integration organizations that have ratified it. They review the implementation of the Convention and any other legal instruments that the COP adopts and make decisions

necessary to promote the effective implementation of the Convention, including institutional and administrative arrangements

Convention
A convention is a multilateral instrument of a lawmaking, codifying, or regulatory nature. Conventions are usually negotiated under the auspices of international entities or a conference of states

Declaration
The term "declaration" is used to indicate that the parties do not intend to create binding obligations but merely want to declare certain aspirations

Deposit
After a treaty has been concluded, the written instruments, which provide formal evidence of consent to be bound, and also reservations and declarations, are placed in the custody of a depositary

Ecosystem services
Are the benefits that humans receive from nature. These benefits underpin almost every aspect of human well-being, including our food and water, security, health, and economy

Entry into Force
Coming into legal effect of an international agreement and becomes legally binding for the States that have ratified it or acceded to it. Typically, the provisions of the treaty determine the date on which the treaty enters into force

Heat content The amount of heat energy available to be released by the use of a specified physical unit of an energy form (e.g., a ton of coal, a barrel of oil, a kilowatt-hour of electricity, a cubic foot of natural gas, or a pound of steam)

Indigenous and local knowledge
Refers to the understanding, skills and philosophies developed by societies with long histories of interaction with the national

surrounding. This knowledge is integral to a cultural complex that also encompass language, systems of classification, resource use practices, social interaction, ritual and spirituality

Jurisdiction
Territory within which a court or government agency may properly exercise its power

Nature-based Solutions
Nature-based Solutions leverage nature and the power of healthy ecosystems to protect people, optimize infrastructure, and safeguard a stable and biodiverse future

Omic
The word omics refers to a field of study in biological sciences that ends with -*omics*, such as genomics, transcriptomics, proteomics, or metabolomics

Protocol
An agreement less formal than a 'treaty' or 'convention'. A protocol signifies an instrument that creates legally binding obligations of international law. In most cases this term encompasses an instrument which is a subsidiary to a treaty

Ratification
Ratification defines the international act whereby a state indicates its consent to be bound to a treaty

Satoyama
In Japanese, Satoyama refers to managed woodlands or grasslands (*yama*) adjacent to villages (*sato*)

Stakeholders
A stakeholder is a person, group, or organization with a vested interest or stake in the decision-making and activities of a business, organization, or project

Sovereignty
Sovereignty is a political concept that refers to dominant power or supreme authority. In a monarchy, supreme power

resides in the "sovereign" or king. In democracies, sovereign power rests with the people and is exercised through representative bodies such as Congress or Parliament

Treaty
A binding formal agreement, contract, or other written instrument that establishes obligations between two or more subjects of international law (primarily states and international organizations

Suggestions for Further Readings

Native American Wisdom

All Great Quotes. *Native American.* https://www.allgreatquotes.com/protect-the-forests-for-our-children/.

Brainy Quotes. *Chief Seattle Quotes.* https://www.brainyquote.com/authors/chief-seattle-quotes

Goodreads. *Dan George Quotes.* https://www.goodreads.com/author/quotes/644321.Dan_George.

Passionate People

Borgese, E.M. (1985). *The Future of the Ocean: A Report to the Club of Rome.* Harvest House.

Borgese, E. M. (1998). *The Oceanic Circle.* United Nations University Press.

Borgese, E. M. (1977). *La Planète Mer.* Seuil edition.

Borgese, E. M, & Facey, L. (1994). *Chairworm & supershark.* The Mill Press.

BirdLife. *We are a global family of 123 national Partners covering all continents, landscapes and seascapes.* https://www.birdlife.org/how-we-work/.

Carson, R. (1950). *The See Around Us.* Oxford University Press

Carson, R. (1955). *The Edge of the Sea*: First Marine Books

Carson, R. (1952) *Under the Sea Wind.* Penguin Classics.

Carson, R. (1962) *Silent Spring, and Other Writings on the Environment*: Library of America.

CONSERVATION INTERNATIONAL. McCoy M. K. (2024) Study: How nature can fight climate change — and how it can't

E.O. Wilson Biodiversity Foundation. *Why Half?.* Why Half? - E.O. Wilson Biodiversity Foundation.

Figueres, C., Robert-Carnac, T. (2020). *The Future we Choose: Surviving the Climate Crisis.* Knopf.

Greenpeace. *Preserve, protect and restore our planet.* Nature - Greenpeace International.

International Ocean Institute (IOI). *The Founder of IOI: Elisabeth Mann Borgese.* https://www.ioinst.org/elisabeth-mann-borgese/.

IUCN. *Biodiversity. IUCN monitors species and ecosystems, and steers policy and action to protect and restore the natural world.* https://iucn.org/our-work/biodiversity.

IUCN Red List. *Wandering Albatross.* Diomedea exulans (Wandering Albatross).

National Geographic Society. (1983). *People's and Places of the Past. The Dawn of Humanity.* The National Geographic Illustrated Cultural Atlas of the Ancient World, pages 8-19.

The Nature Conservancy. *Conserving Fresh Water for Life on Earth.* It's Time to Protect Fresh Water for People and Nature | TNC.

Tollefson, J. (2015). *CHRISTIANA FIGUERES: Climate guardian. A dynamic leader charted the path to a new global climate agreement* 365 days: *Nature*'s 10 volume 528, pages 459–467

Wilson, E. O. (2016). *Half-Earth: Our Planet's Fight for Life.* Liveright.

World Wildlife Fund (WWF). Johanson, M. (2024). Promoting tradition and fostering ecotourism | Stories | WWF.

(WWF). *Wildlife Conservation Conserve threatened wildlife and wild places to sustain life on Earth.* https://www.worldwildlife.org/initiatives/wildlife-conservation.

First Agreements to Protect Life on Earth

Convention on the Conservation of Migratory Species of Wild Animals (CMS) 1979. https://www.cms.int/en/species.

Convention on International Trade in Endangered Species of Wild
Fauna and Flora (CITES). https://cites.org/eng/disc/what.php

Convention on Wetlands (RAMSAR) *The importance of wetlands.*
https://www.ramsar.org/

International Plant Protection Convention (IPPC).
https://www.ippc.int/en/history-of-the-ippc/.

International Whaling Commission (IWC). https://iwc.int/en/.

Perry, A. K. (2023). *How whaling works.* HowStuffWorks
Science.https://science.howstuffworks.com/environmental/
conservation/issues/whaling4.htm.

United Nations Educational, Scientific and Cultural Organization
(UNESCO). *We bring people and nations together through
education, culture and science.* https://www.unesco.org/en.

RAMSAR. *Global Wetland Outlook.* https://www.global-wetland-
outlook.ramsar.org/

First Conference on Human Environment

United Nations Sustainable Development. *Report of the World
Commission on Environment Development: Our Common Future.*
*https://sustainabledevelopment.un.org/content/documents/5987our-
common-future.pdf*

United Nations (UN). *United Nations Conference on the human
environment, Stockholm 1972. United Nations.*
https://www.un.org/en/conferences/environment/stockholm1972.

World Commission on Environment Development (1987) *Our
Common Future.* Oxford University Press.

IUCN *World Conservation Strategy..*https://portals.iucn.org/library/
efiles/documents/wcs-004.pdf

Protection of Marine Life

Chavez, F.P., R.J. Miller, F.E. Muller-Karger, K. Iken, G. Canonico,
K. Egan, J. Price, and W. Turner. 2021. MBON—Marine Biodiversity
Observation Network: An observing system for life in the sea.

Oceanography 34(2):12–15, https://tos.org/oceanography/assets/docs/34-2_chavez1.pdf

IUCN. *Oceans and coasts. IUCN works to conserve coastal, marine and polar ecosystems, and the many benefits they provide for humanity.* https://www.iucn.org/theme/marine-and-polar/our-work/international-ocean-governance.

Marine Biodiversity Observation Network (MBON). https://marinebon.org/

Muller-Karger, F., Canonico, G., Baron, C. Bax, N. , Appeltans, W. Yarincik, K., Leopardas, V., Sousa-Pinto, I., Nakaoka, M., Aikappu, A,. Giddens, J.,Heslop, E., Montes, E., Duffy, J.E. (2022). *Marine Life 2030: building global knowledge of marine life for local action in the Ocean Decade.* ICES Journal of Marine Science, Volume 80, Issue 2, March 2023, Pages 355–357. https://doi.org/10.1093/icesjms/fsac084.

Global Ocean Observing System (GOOS). https://goosocean.org/

National Oceanic and Atmospheric Administration (NOAA). *What is the "EEZ"?* Ocean Exploration. https://oceanexplorer.noaa.gov/facts/useez.html

Ocean Biodiversity Information System (OBIS). https://obis.org/

UNESCO, United Nation Decade for Ocean Science for Sustainable Development (2023) *Vision & Mission. Achieving the ocean we want by 2030*, Paris. https://oceandecade.org/vision-mission/.

UN. Oceans and the Law of the Sea. https://www.un.org/depts/los/

UN. (2002). *Oceans: The source of Life. United Nations Convention on the Law of The Sea, 20th Anniversary* (1982-2002). https://www.un.org/depts/los/convention_agreements/convention_20years/oceanssourceoflife.pdf

Summits for Development and Conservation

Betteli, P. (2021). IISD Earth Negotiation Bulletin What the World Learned Setting Development Goals, 10 pages. https://www.iisd.org/system/files/2021-01/still-one-earth-MDG-SDG.pdf

UN. (1992). *United Nation Conference on Environment and Development, Rio de Janeiro, Brazil, 3-14 June 1992.* https://www.un.org/en/conferences/environment/rio1992

UN. (1992). *Conferences Small Island Developing States.* https://www.un.org/en/conferences/small-islands

UN. (1992). *Agenda 21.* Sustainable Development. https://sustainabledevelopment.un.org/content/documents/Agenda21.pdf

UN. *Take Action for the Sustainable Development Goals* https://www.un.org/sustainabledevelopment/sustainable-development-goals/

UN. (1992). United Nations Convention to Combat Desertification (UNCCD). https://www.unccd.int/convention/overview.

UN. (2000). *Millennium Summit, 6-8 September 2000. New York.* https://www.un.org/en/conferences/environment/newyork2000.

UN. (2012). *United Nations Conference on Sustainable Development, 20-22 June 2012, Rio de Janeiro.* https://www.un.org/en/conferences/environment/rio2012.

UN. (2015). *United Nations Summit on Sustainable Development, 25-27 September 2015, New York.* https://www.un.org/en/conferences/environment/newyork2015

UN. (2015). *THE 17 GOALS.* Department of Economic and Social Affairs. Sustainable Development. https://sdgs.un.org/goals

UN. (2002). *Report of The World Summit on Sustainable Development. Johannesburg, South Africa, 26 August - 4 September 2002.* https://undocs.org/en/A/CONF.199/20

Conservation of Biological Diversity

Active Wilde (2022). *Antarctic Animals List with Pictures & Facts, Species Found In Antarctica.* https://www.activewild.com/antarctic-animals-list/

Active Wilde *(2019). Arctic Animals List with Pictures & Facts: Discover Amazing Animals that Life In the Arctic & Sub-Arctic* https://www.activewild.com/arctic-animals-list/

Business for Nature. (2022). *Financing Our Survivable: Building a Nature Positive Economy through Subside Reform.* https://www.businessfornature.org/news/subsidy-reform

Convention on Biological Diversity (CBD). https://www.cbd.int

(CBD). *Aichi Biodiversity Targets Task Force.* https://www.cbd.int/2011-2020/actors/abttf.

CBD. *Biodiversity and Sustainable Development (2002) CBD News Supplement.* https://www.cbd.int/doc/newsletters/news-sd-suplement-en.pdf.

CBD. (2024).. *BIODIVERSITY COP 16: IMPORTANT AGREEMENTS REACHED TOWARDS MAKING PEACE WITH NATURE.* https://www.cbd.int/article/agreement-reached-cop-16

CBD. BIOSAFETY PROTOCOL NEWS. *National and Regional Celebrations:20th anniversary of the entry into force of the Cartagena Protocol on Biosafety* Latest Issue: No. 19 – 2024 https://bch.cbd.int/protocol/cpb_newsletter.shtml.

CBD. Booklets and Brochures. https://www.cbd.int/programmes/outreach/awareness/publications.shtml?grp=xc.

CBD. *History of the Convention (2004) News Special Edition.* https://www.cbd.int/doc/publications/CBD-10th-anniversary.pdf.

CBD. *Japan Biodiversity Fund.* https://www.cbd.int/jbf/about/.

CBD. Kan, Naoto: *Towards societies in harmony with nature 2010* Secretariat of the Convention on Biological Diversity pp 4-5. https://www.cbd.int/doc/newsletters/satoyama/cbd-satoyama-2010-en.pdf.

CBD. *Kunming-Montreal Global Biodiversity Framework (GBF).* https://www.cbd.int/gbf.

CBD. National Biodiversity Strategies and Action Plans (NBSAPs https://www.cbd.int/nbsap/.

CBD. *PERIODICAL PUBLICATIONS.* https://www.cbd.int/doc/newsletters

CBD. (2015). *Priority Actions to Achieve Aichi Target 10 for Coral Reefs and Closely Related Ecosystem.* https://www.cbd.int/doc/publications/cbd-aichi-target-10-en.pdf.

CBD Secretariat. (2023). Tristan, T. *The Kunming-Montreal Global Biodiversity Framework Oceans & Climate Change.* https://unfccc.int/sites/default/files/resource/OD2023Day1_CBD.pdf.

CBD. Secretariat of the Convention on Biological Diversity (2020). Global Biodiversity Outlook 5. Montreal. https://www.cbd.int/gbo/gbo5/publication/gbo-5-en.pdf.

CBD. (2010). *Strategic Plan for Biodiversity 2011–2020 and the Aichi Targets "Living in Harmony with Nature.* https://www.cbd.int/doc/strategic-plan/2011-2020/aichi-targets-en.pdf.

CBD (2000) *Sustaining life on Earth. How the Convention on Biological Diversity promotes nature and human well-being.* https://www.cbd.int/convention/guide/default.shtml?id=next.

CBC. (2030). *The Biodiversity Plan for Life on Earth Targets Quick Access.*https://www.cbd.int/gbf/targets/1/

CBC. *The Cartagena Protocol on Biosafety.* https://bch.cbd.int/protocol/.

CBC. *The Nagoya Protocol on Access and Benefit-sharing.* https://www.cbd.int/abs.

CBD. *2011-2020 United Nations Decade on Biodiversity. Living in harmony with nature.*https://www.cbd.int/2011-2020/.

Chan, L., Hillel, O., Werner, P., Holman, N., Coetzee, I., Galt, R., and Elmqvist, T. 2021 *Handbook on the Singapore Index on Cities' Biodiversity (also known as the City Biodiversity Index).* Montreal: Secretariat of the Convention on Biological Diversity and Singapore: National Parks Board, Singapore. 70 Pages. https://www.cbd.int/doc/publications/cbd-ts-98-en.pdf.

EPA. Ecosystem Services Enviro Atlas. *What are ecosystem services, and why are they important?* Last updated on August 21, 2024 https://www.epa.gov/enviroatlas/ecosystem-services-enviroatlas-1

FAO, IFAD, UNICEF, WFP and WHO. 2022. *The State of Food Security and Nutrition in the World 2022. Repurposing food and agricultural policies to make healthy diets more affordable.* Rome, FAO. https://doi.org/10.4060/cc0639en.

Gentili, R., Schaffner, U., Martinoli, A,.Citterio, S,.(2021) Invasive alien species and biodiversity: Impacts and management, Biodiversity, 22:1-2, 1-3, DOI: 10.1080/14888386.2021.1929484

Global Youth Biodiversity Network (2016) *CBD in a Nutshell. Global Youth Biodiversity Network. Germany.* https://www.cbd.int/youth/doc/cbd_in_a_nutshell.pdf

Government of Canada Publications. (2020). *Biodiversity Goals and Targets for Canada 2020* BiodivCanada Cat. No.:CW66-524/2016E-PDF ISBN: 978-0-660-04248-. https://www.biodivcanada.ca/.

Island Nature Trust. Smith. An Introduction to Ecosystems Services. https://islandnaturetrust.ca/introduction-to-ecosystem-services.

IPBES. *The thematic assessment report on THE SUSTAINABLE USE OF WILD SPECIES SUMMARY FOR POLICYMAKERS* https://www.biodic.go.jp/biodiversity/about/ipbes/deliverables/files/EN_SPM_SUSTAINABLE_USE_OF_WILD_SPECIES.pdf

IUCN. (2023). *Embracing biodiversity: Paving the way for nature-inclusive cities.* https://www.iucn.org/story/202305/embracing-biodiversity-paving-way-nature-inclusive-cities.

Organization for Economic Cooperation and Development OECD (2020) *A Comprehensive Overview of Global Biodiversity Finance.* https://www.oecd.org/environment/resources/biodiversity/report-a-comprehensive-overview-of-global-biodiversity-finance.pdf

ResearchGate (2015*).* Laird, S*. Access and Benefit Sharing: Key Points for Policy Makers - Industrial Biotechnology.* https://www.researchgate.net/profile/Sarah-Laird-6/publication/303315642_Access_and_Benefit_Sharing_

UNDP (2021) *Access to Genetic Resources and Benefit Sharing. Theory to Practice under the Nagoya Protocol.* https://www.undp.org/publications/access-genetic-resources-and-benefit-sharing-theory-practice-under-nagoya-protocol

UNEP 2022) *Integrated Spatial Planning Workbook.* *https://www.undp.org/sites/g/files/zskgke326/files/2022-12/UNDP-GEF-Integrated-Spatial-Planning-Workbook.pdf*

UNEP (2022) *UN Biodiversity Conference (COP 15)* https://www.unep.org/un-biodiversity-conference-cop-15

UNDP-SCBD & UNEP-WCMC (2021) *Creating a Nature-Positive Future. The opportunity and contribution of protected areas and other effective area-based conservation measures.* https://www.undp.org/sites/g/files/zskgke326/files/2021-11/UNDP-UNEP-Creating-a-Nature-Positive-Future-EN.pdf.

United Nations Environment Programme (2022). *Nature-based Solutions: Opportunities and Challenges for Scaling Up.* https://wedocs.unep.org/20.500.11822/40783.

WHOI (2020) *New study takes comprehensive look at Marine pollution. https://www.whoi.edu/press-room/news-release/ comprehensive-look-at-marine-pollution-2/*

Women4Biodiversity. *Advancing Women's Rights, Gender Equality and the Future of Biodiversity in the Post-2020 Global Biodiversity Framework (2021).* https://www.women4biodiversity.org/advancing-womens-rights-gender-equality-and-the-future-of-biodiversity/

Yong, Ed (2023) *An Immense World. How Animals Senses Reveal the Hidden Realms Around Us.* Random House Trade

Climate Change

Care about Climate. (2020) Benduski, M. *Paris Agreement vs Kyoto Protocol [Comparison Chart]*https://www.careaboutclimate.org/blog/paris-agreement-vs-kyoto-protocol-comparison-chart.

Climate Champions UNFCCC. *RACE TO ZERO. The world's largest coalition of non-state actors taking immediate action to halve global emissions by 2030.* https://climatechampions.unfccc.int/system/race-to-zero.

Climate Champions UNFCCC. *2030 Breakthroughs: Upgrading our Systems Together: A global challenge to accelerate sector breakthroughs for COP26 – and beyond.* https://climatechampions.unfccc.int/system/breakthroughs/.

Climate Champions UNFCCC. *THE SHARM-EL-SHEIKH ADAPTATION AGENDA.* https://climatechampions.unfccc.int/system/sharm-el-sheikh-adaptation-agenda/.

COP28 United Arab Emirates UAE. (2023). *COALITION FOR HIGH AMBITION MULTILEVEL PARTNERSHIPS CHAMP) FOR CLIMATE ACTION* https://www.cop28.com/en/cop28-uae-coalition-for-high-ambition-multilevel-partnerships-for-climate-action.

National Advisory Committee for Aeronautics (NASA), (2019) *New Studies Increase Confidence in NASA's Measure of Earth's Temperature.* https://climate.nasa.gov/news/2876/new-studies-increase-confidence-in-nasas-measure-of-earths-temperature/.

United Nations Framework Convention on Climate Change (UNFCCC). *What is the United Nations Framework Convention on Climate Change?* https://unfccc.int/process-and-meetings/what-is-the-united-nations-framework-convention-on-climate-change.

UNFCCC. (1997). *What is the Kyoto Protocol?.* https://unfccc.int/kyoto_protocol.

UNFCCC. (2015). *Key aspects of the Paris Agreement.* https://unfccc.int/most-requested/key-aspects-of-the-paris-agreement.

UNFCCC. (2016)..*Marrakech Partnership for Global Climate Action.* https://unfccc.int/climate-action/engagement/marrakech-partnership

UNFCCC. (2020). *The Glasgow Climate Pact – Key Outcomes from COP26.* https://unfccc.int/process-and-meetings/the-paris-agreement/the-glasgow-climate-pact-key-outcomes-from-cop26.

UNFCCC. (2022). *Five Key Takeaways from COP27.* https://unfccc.int/process-and-meetings/conferences/sharm-el-sheikh-climate-change-conference-november-2022/five-key-takeaways-from-cop27

UNFCCC. (2023). *COP 28: What Was Achieved and What Happens Next?* https://unfccc.int/cop28/5-key-takeaways.

UNFCCC. (2024). *UN Climate Change Conference Baku - COP29.* https://unfccc.int/.

UN. (2024). *COP29 concludes with climate finance deal.* https://www.un.org/en/climatechange/cop29

Ocean Pavillon. (2023). *COP28 Dubai Ocean Declaration.* https://oceanpavilion-cop.org/dubai-ocean-declaration

Ocean Pavillon. (2024). *COP29 Baku Ocean Declaration* https://oceanpavilion-cop.org/baku-ocean-declaration/#signatories

Acknowledgements

It was a big task to offer any lecturer, a comprehensive summary of the challenge and solutions, humanity is facing this Millennium. I am indebted to Dr Hamdallah Zedan former Secretary of the Convention to Biodiversity, Juan Mayr former Chairman of the Cartagena Protocol, and Ms. Jyoti Mathur-Filipp, former Director for Implementation at the secretariat of the Convention on Biological Diversity (CBD) for their encouragement and support.

I express my deepest gratitude to Frank Müller-Karger, Professor at University of South Florida, College of Marine Science for his friendly and knowledgeable guidance through the protection of marine life chapter and to Francisco Arias Isaza, Director of INVEMAR, for emboldening me throughout my work.

Also, my gratitude to others specialists: Michel Besner, former Marine Biology Researcher, Carolina Cáceres, Director International Biodiversity Environment and Climate Change Canada, Jean-Marc Gagnon, Scientific Director of the Canadian Nature Museum, Antonella Vassallo, Managing Director International Ocean Institute Headquarters, Martin Savard, Educator at the Federation québécoise des chasseurs et pêcheurs,. They all took time to read chapters of this publication and offered comments based on their expertise.

I could not have completed this digital book without the generous help of Anne Dwart and Bilyana Ilievska for the English review.

My thanks to all of you.

Gloria Rodríguez Zuleta

Credit photographs

Made in United States
Orlando, FL
14 December 2024

55723933R00066